KU-467-663

CONTENTS

BOWS AGAINST THE BARONS

BOWS AGAINST
THE BARONS

Geoffrey Trease

Illustrated by

C. Walter Hodges

Elliott & Thompson
London

Chapter One

Merrie England

Crack!

The long whip curled round his shoulders, burning the flesh under his ragged tunic. Dickon swayed sickly, but did not cry out. His hands tightened on the woollen cap he held, and he bit his lip to still the pain.

'I'll have no idlers,' said the bailiff.

He glared down at the boy, a mountainous man on a mountainous horse, his hard face dark with passion.

'That'll teach you to fail in your duties, my lad. You know what they are well enough. Repeat them.'

Dickon looked up sullenly. His blood boiled within him. He longed to leap on the bailiff's saddle-bow and drive his dagger into that fat belly, but he knew how impossible it was. The man would shake him off like a rat, and the long sword would flash down to finish him for ever....

It was no good. The masters were the masters. The peasants must obey and be whipped and work again, till death brought time for resting.

'Yes, sir,' he answered between clenched teeth. 'I must work on my lord's land every other day; I must plough four acres of his land in the springtime and furnish two oxen for the work; I must –'

'That'll do,' interrupted Master William harshly. 'Why weren't you at work this morning?'

'It was the pig, sir. It had strayed into the forest. If I hadn't gone to look for it –' He broke off with an appealing look. 'It is the only pig we have, sir.'

'Pigs? What the devil do I care about your pigs?' The horseman raised his whip again menacingly. 'You are all pigs, you labourers. Next week you will work on the lord's land every day as a punishment.' He wheeled his horse in the sandy track. Once more Dickon longed to plunge his knife into that fleshy body. 'Mind you're there,' the bailiff shouted over his shoulder, 'or I'll have you flogged.' He cantered away to inspect the work at the mill.

Miserably, Dickon walked on towards the mud-and-straw hovel which he called home. It had been a long, tiring day, toiling on the miserable strips of land held by his father, and he had not yet a man's strength.

If only his father would return! But he had been gone for years now, along with Sir Rolf and the other fighting men of the estate. They had gone overseas to the Holy Land, some said to keep Jerusalem against the heathen, others to win plunder and power from anyone, heathen or Christian, who happened to be weaker than they.

Dickon wished his father would come back to work the land with him, or that he himself had been old enough to join Sir Rolf as an archer and venture overseas.

Anything would be better than this endless drudgery, slaving to keep himself, his mother, and his younger brothers alive. Easy for the bailiff to ride about, fat with good food and drink and sleep! He didn't know what it was to sweat, except with too much flesh. Nor to go hungry and cold and wet, never knowing when a whip was going to snake round your shoulders.

'Good evening, young Dickon,' said a suave voice at his side.

He turned. The village priest stood smiling at him, but with an unpleasant glint in his beady black eyes. Dickon pulled off his cap quickly and bobbed respectfully. One must not offend the priests.

'Good evening, Father,' he answered, and nothing in his tone betrayed that of all people, after the bailiff, the priest was the one he was most anxious to avoid.

'You have not paid your full tithe, my lad,' said the other, toying with the crucifix which dangled at his waist.

'No.' Dickon flushed. He had known this must come sooner or later. 'It has been a bad year, Father.

Some of my hens died in the flood. And the crops were poor. We have hardly enough to live on ourselves –'

'Nevertheless, one-tenth is owed to Mother Church.' The priest rolled his eyes piously to heaven. 'That must come first, lad. It may be a little, but in the eyes of God –' His voice took on the sing-song tone he used in church 'You remember the story of the widow's mite?'

'We can't pay,' said Dickon stubbornly. 'My mother is ill, because we have not enough to eat. I'm not strong enough to work the land as my father does. We're too poor.'

'Blessed are the poor!' chanted the priest, clasping his smooth white hands.

'You're not poor,' muttered the boy, 'or you wouldn't say that.'

'Dickon!' The man's tone changed sharply. 'You forget you are speaking to a servant of God. Pay your tithe by next week, or the Church's officers will come to seize it.'

'Let them seize what they can,' said Dickon bitterly. He thrust his cap back on his unruly black hair, and strode off down the road again. The priest stood speechless with anger, watching his retreating figure with eyes which betokened him no good in the future.

Evening was falling and already the sun had gone, leaving the western sky red above the countless tree-tops of the forest. Out of the gloom a few low houses showed along the side of the road, a glow of fire lighting up their open doorways. Ducks were swimming in the stream and a herd of pigs were rooting about for acorns at the fringe of the woodland.

Dickon passed by the cottages, calling a good night to those who stood round their doors. His own home was at the far end of the village, a stone's-throw from the rest. It was almost overshadowed by the great oaks of the forest. Only a thin strip of cherished garden, with carefully planted vegetables and a couple of beehives, separated the hut from the boundless expanses of Sherwood.

'You're late, lad,' said his mother.

She was a tired, grey little woman, worn out by too much work and too little food. She put a wooden platter in front of him bearing a mess of steaming vegetables. He seized an oatcake and began to munch it before replying.

'Bailiff's been after me,' he grunted through a mouthful of supper. 'And priest too – about the tithe.'

His mother sighed. In the shadowy corner of the hut the pale faces of his brothers lifted from the rags under which they were sleeping. Three pairs of anxious eyes were fixed on Dickon, three pairs of ears strained to hear what new trouble was about to fall upon the family.

'If only Dad would come home,' went on Dickon savagely, 'instead of gallivanting about in foreign parts –'

'You mustn't say that. Your father didn't want to go. He had to. None of them wanted to. But a hundred were taken, all the best archers. And where are they now? Dead, most like. Killed by blackamoors or at the bottom of the sea.' His mother dashed away a tear from her weathered cheek. Dickon patted her shoulder.

'There, Mother. We'll manage somehow. We can

pay the priest if we scrape, but it won't leave us much food for ourselves.'

'No. Have you seen what the deer have done outside?'

'No.' Dickon frowned. 'Have they been at the crops again?'

'Ay. They've rooted up a lot and trampled more. A month's food destroyed in a night.'

Dickon swore one of his rare oaths. 'I'd like to put an arrow through one of the beasts! Then we'd have venison, for once, and our vegetables too.'

'Hush!' She peered out of the doorway into the gathering darkness. 'Someone might hear you. You know what it means to touch the King's deer!'

'Well, why can't the King keep them off our fields? He comes here about once a year to hunt – and all the rest of the time they trample our crops and eat our roots and undo all the work we do. And we're not allowed to do a thing. We can starve, but the deer grow fat. It's not right.'

'It's always been so,' said his mother sadly, 'and I suppose it always will be. So long as we keep alive somehow, to do their work and fight their wars, they don't care how poor we are.'

'I'd like to teach them!'

She smiled. 'Boy's words! You'll learn to take your whip and be thankful. Better that than lose your ears or be hanged from an oak-tree. You'd better go to sleep now. There's plenty to do tomorrow.'

The fire was already out, quenched when the curfew-bell rang out from the church tower. It was dark and the full moon not yet risen. Dickon stretched his weary body on a pile of dried bracken near the doorway and was soon asleep.

His dreams were troubled. He saw again the faces of the bailiff and the priest threatening him. He dreamt it was winter again, and no food in the hut. And game, juicy meat, in the shape of hares and rabbits and birds and deer played tantalizingly on the fringe of the forest, where it was forbidden to carry an arrow, let alone shoot one.

It was long after midnight when he awoke, for the moonlight was pouring in through the hole in the roof which served as chimney. He was dreaming confusedly of charging horsemen, who began by chasing deer and ended by pursuing himself. He started up, the sound of hoofs on the ground echoing in his ears.

He listened for a moment. It was no dream. The noise came from outside the hut. He caught up his bow and arrows, flung open the door, and looked out.

A whole herd of deer had just cantered out of the woodland and was now contentedly feasting upon his cabbages! As he watched, a week's food for the family vanished before his eyes.

This was too much. Thoughtlessly, madly, he notched an arrow on the string, drew it back to his ear, and let fly at the leader.

True to aim, the long shaft buried itself in the beast's throat. The hart leapt in the air, fell over, and drummed its hoofs on the earth for a moment. Then its head rolled limply on its neck, and it lay still.

The rest of the deer had vanished like shadows into the greater shadow of the forest. He was alone with the dead hart under the moon.

He stepped forward and examined his kill. Then

he brushed his bloodstained hand slowly across his brow. Gradually he realized the terrible thing he had done.

He had killed one of the King's deer!

A cold sweat started out on his forehead, where his hand had left a smear of blood. He stood as though petrified, wondering what to do.

Everything in the forest was sacred to the King. To fell a tree was a crime, even to cut a branch.... As for shooting one of the deer! Even an earl might do it only by royal permission. A common man would be more likely to lose his ears or one of his hands.

Dickon shivered. His friends might joke that his ears stuck out and were over-large, but he had no desire to part with them. As for losing a hand, what use would he be to anyone afterwards?

No, they wouldn't cut off a hand, because he wouldn't be any use to Sir Rolf if they did. He was Sir Rolf's serf, Sir Rolf's property. It didn't matter about his own work, but they'd have to leave him fit to work for Sir Rolf.

It would probably be his ears, he decided.

Unless –

He looked round hopelessly. No chance of concealing his crime. He would need help to drag the deer away. Other people would know then, and talk. The King's foresters had eyes and ears everywhere.

Only in the forest would he be safe. Sherwood was the poor man's refuge. Folk said it was full of outlaws, old soldiers who had no work, escaped serfs and men who had broken the law – desperate men who would as soon slit his throat as take him for their comrade.

Only Robin Hood was different. If he could find Robin Hood and take service under him, in the band of which village folk spoke admiringly but in cautious whispers....

Dickon looked at the forest. It looked mysterious and forbidding, so dark compared with the open field that was silver under the moon. There were wolves, wild boars, and desperate men. Somewhere, if he still existed, was Robin Hood, but to find him in this maze of wood and heath would be like searching for a needle in a haystack.

Yet he must go. He waited no longer. Stealing back to the hut, he groped for his cap, his dagger, and his few other possessions. He was careful not to wake his mother. If she knew nothing, they would not punish her.

For food he took only a couple of oatcakes in his wallet, but as he passed the hart, he bent, smiling, and cut himself a piece of the meat. If he was to be outlawed, he might as well taste the venison!

Then, with a last glance at the village, he slipped noiselessly into the forest.

Chapter Two

Outlawed

Dickon's first concern was to get clear away from Oxton, his home, before morning broke. Finding the outlaw leader would have to wait, if necessary, for days or even weeks. Indeed, it was more than successive sheriffs and head foresters had managed to accomplish in twenty or thirty years, but Dickon hoped to be more lucky. Alone and unarmed save for his bow and knife, he did not look like an officer of the law, and he felt sure that sooner or later he would fall in with someone who would direct him to the band.

Sherwood was no continuous stretch of dense forest. In places the oaks stood well apart, the ground beneath them green with short turf and moss. Elsewhere, taller and straighter trees clustered like silver lances in the moonlight, or clumps of fir and holly presented thickets too dark and impenetrable for a pathway. Sometimes he would come on a spacious clearing, carpeted with green bracken, knee high and more. The scene was always changing, and no two spots looked alike.

One or two roads, worn down to the bare, sandy soil, crossed the forest from side to side, and these were most to be avoided. There were 'rides' too – broad green tracks, cut like slashes straight through the woods. In the daytime he must keep off these too, lest he meet patrolling foresters.

Dawn was coming. He marked the creeping white light directly behind him, and was relieved to find that he had not lost direction. Oxton lay on the eastward fringe of the forest. He was heading right away from it and into the heart of the woodland.

He left the open ride now and struck through the undergrowth, moving as silently as he could and skirting all clearings lest, by bad luck, there should be eyes to see him as he crossed.

He was hungry, but the dry oatcake choked him. He must search for a stream to drink, before he could eat. The venison, too, must wait. He dared not risk a fire whose smell or smoke might betray his whereabouts.

If only it had been late summer or autumn! There would have been berries in plenty to moisten his mouth. But it was barely June, and he found nothing but a couple of whitish, under-sized strawberries, growing on a bank.

Once he startled a herd of deer. They rose from the tall bracken, took one look at him with their mild eyes, and turned tail. He heard them crashing through the undergrowth, saw their dappled bodies merge into the light-and-shade pattern of the leaves.

From close at hand came a laugh, and another voice laughing in answer.

Dickon sank into the deep foliage and lay absolutely still, hand on dagger, ears straining in the direction of the sounds.

He could hear the soft footfalls of horses sinking in the loose sand of a forest track. Then came a jingle of harness. He crouched closer under the bracken-fronds. Outlaws did not go mounted along the highways....

'I could wish the trees bore more of such fruit,' said an unpleasant voice nearer than ever.

'Ay, so could I,' was the answer from another of the unseen horsemen.

Closer and closer came the trampling hoofs. The bridles seemed to jingle in his very ears. In another moment it seemed they would be riding over the spot where he lay. Stealthily, he drew the keen dagger from its sheath.

To be in the forest, even, with bow and arrows was an offence against the law! Anyone who saw him would arrest him, he would be handed over to the foresters – and then there would be a reckoning for last night's kill.

It seemed like an age. Cautiously he raised himself on one elbow and peered through the screen of leaves. Just as he did so, the riders passed across his line of vision, not twenty yards away. He could see only their heads and shoulders.

There were four of them, and they wore helmets and the livery of a baron on the other side of the forest. Dickon laughed in his heart. They would have little chance of catching him in the woods, these heavily armoured men on their huge war-horses. But if he had stumbled on the road before them, it would have been a different matter. He shivered, imagining how they would have charged down on him, and their lances would have run clean through his back between the shoulder blades.

They rode by, joking and never gazing aside into the bracken from which the boy's brown face was peering. When they had disappeared, he lay still and considered.

A main highway, whose existence he had not suspected, ran straight across his line of flight. It would be a busy one, leading to the town of Nottingham. Quite a stream of traffic would be going up and down – merchants with their pack-horses, pedlars, friars, soldiers, and others.

None of these must see him. They would remember a boy, travelling alone, for no one went singly on a forest trail. He would be reported to the foresters....

Cautiously he wormed his way forward to the verge of the undergrowth. A great stretch of open track and turf separated him from the safety of the other side.

Raising his head, he looked up and down the road – and what he saw caused his stomach to rise within him.

For there was only a human figure in view, and he was dead – very horribly dead.

A short stone's-throw from Dickon's hiding-place he hung, turning slowly in the breeze, from the outstretched arm of an oak. Ten feet above the ground he swung, handless and grinning, now little more than a bundle of bones and rags.

This was the 'fruit' of which the soldier had wanted to see a bigger crop!

Once it had been a man, whose only crimes had been that he was not born rich and noble, and that he had stolen rather than starve. Now he was a scarecrow to frighten others who might rebel, 'forest fruit' for the hirelings of the rich to laugh at.

Without caring any more whether he was seen or not, Dickon ran blindly across the road and plunged into the woods on the other side. On and on he rushed, tripping over roots and twining creepers, once stumbling knee-deep into a slimy pool. At last, when he was too breathless to run any more, he slowed down, panting, to a walk.

There was a stream here, and he flung himself down on the grass, drinking from the cup made by his hands. He was faint, but had no desire to eat now. The sight of the dead man would have taken any appetite away.

All that day he wandered on, avoiding tracks and signs of habitation, keeping to the densest thickets, and starting at every sudden noise.

The forest was getting on his nerves. It was so vast and empty. He must have walked fifteen miles in it, and there was no sign of outlaws.

Perhaps Robin Hood was dead. Or perhaps he had gone north to the mountains men said lay beyond the boundaries of Sherwood, in far-away Yorkshire.

Was Dickon doomed to remain alone, every man's hand against him? It was not a pleasant thought.

He began to long for sunset. Night would bring safety. True, the forest had its wild beasts, wolves and boars, but they were seldom fierce in summer. And he would be able to light a fire without the smoke giving him away.

Slowly, ever so slowly, the sun sank in the western sky. It was twilight under the trees, but above them it was still bright. Not until he could see nothing but blue, and the first stars were beginning to come out, did he dare to use his flint and tinder.

He had found a sheltered little dell, close hidden by a thicket through which he had crawled on hands and knees. The fire he lit so low in the hollow that not even the highest flame would show more than twenty yards away. Here, surely, he would be quite safe till morning.

He skewered the venison on a sharp piece of wood and turned it in the flames. The smell made him almost mad with hunger, and it was hateful to see the grease dripping into the fire and being wasted. Every now and again he ran his finger along the browning joint and sucked it.

At last the meat was ready. He cut off a lump with his dagger and ate it in his hands, burning his fingers and throat in his ravenous impatience. He finished one of the oatcakes, but kept one for the next day. Food was a problem he would have to face in earnest.

When his hunger was satisfied he realized suddenly how tired he was, having missed half a night's sleep and walked farther than ever before in his life. He collected as much dry bracken as he could and made up a bed which, if not very soft or comfortable, was at least as good as he was used to. Then he put the cold venison out of reach of animals and insects, lay down, and fell asleep.

Sheer exhaustion kept him in deep sleep until nearly dawn, when the acute chilliness which always comes about that time, even in high summer, began to stir him into wakefulness. He opened his eyes, saw the sky still dark and starry above him, and closed them again, huddling down into the bracken for warmth.

He must be up and away by dawn. But when dawn came he was back in an uneasy sleep, and when the sun rose it was so hot and comfortable that he slept far into the morning.

All around him the forest was awake. Birds were twittering, squirrels running up and down the branches, deer gliding through the brakes, foresters starting their rounds.

Dickon slept on, though every minute added danger. It was only an hour or two to noon when a voice wakened him. He rolled over and reached instinctively for his dagger.

To his horror, the sheath was empty. The bow which had lain beside it was gone.

'Good morning, lad,' said a pleasant voice from behind him.

Dickon turned quickly on his other elbow and sat up. A red-faced man, merry of eye, was watching him from the banks of the dell. Dickon noted that the lean brown hands toyed carelessly with a knife – his knife – and that escape was impossible. Something about the stranger's smile told him that it did not matter.

'It's unhealthy to sleep late in the forest,' said the man reprovingly. 'Where are you going? And what's your name? You needn't answer unless you like, you know, but unless you do I can't give you back your knife.'

This was no forester, Dickon realized. Most of them were French, but this man spoke in the local dialect. And he wore the green Lincoln cloth favoured by those who sought concealment in the greenwood.

He smiled back at the stranger. 'My name's Dickon, son of Dick at Oxton. I made a bit of a mistake. So I'm looking for a friend.'

The outlaw's blue eyes twinkled and his eyebrows rose comically on his sun-tanned forehead.

'Ah! And what might his name be? Perhaps he's a friend of mine, too.'

'Well,' said Dickon slowly, watching his questioner very closely, 'it might be Robin.'

'Robin?' The man scratched his stubby chin. 'Yes. I know a Robin. Now I wonder if it's the same?'

'Hood,' Dickon added boldly. The man slapped his thigh and got up.

'The same! And you want to join him?'

'If he'll have me.'

'If you're the right sort, he will. You look it. But we'll know by tomorrow.'

'How?'

'We find out most things that happen round Sherwood. Especially when folk make mistakes. But if you're a spy sent by the foresters, well –' He paused significantly.

'What then?'

'It would be a pity to see a bonny boy like you swinging from a tree.'

Chapter Three

Comrades of the Forest

'You might help to carry these,' said the outlaw when
Dickon had removed all traces of his camp. He pointed
to a couple of sacks on the ground, which, from their
feel, appeared to contain provisions of various kinds.
Dickon obediently swung one of them over his shoulder and followed his guide from the dell.

There was no talk between them as they went.
The outlaw, from caution perhaps, seemed disin-
clined to speak about himself, and most of the time
they went in single file, threading their way through
the densest parts of the forest.

Dickon admired the sure, silent step of his companion and tried to imitate it. This man was never
doubtful of his way, though at times he paused, nose
in air, like a stag alert for danger. Then he would
move on, or strike off at a tangent. No twigs crack-
led under his feet; the leaves hardly rustled.

They went on for an hour thus, penetrating into
a lonelier part of Sherwood than Dickon had yet
entered. There were no rides here and open glades
were few. Sometimes the outlaw would walk up to an
apparently unbroken mass of thorns and brambles,
part them with a careful hand, and expose a dark little path winding away within. They would bend their
heads and enter, and the briars would close behind
them, baffling the keenest eye.

Once a man in green stepped from behind a tree and greeted them. After a word or two, he walked back into the shadows and in an instant had vanished from view. Dickon peered vainly under the boughs. Neither sight nor sound betrayed the hidden sentinel.

No one else spoke to them as they went on, but all the time the boy had the sense of unseen eyes watching them. He began to notice new bird-notes – notes so natural that they would have deceived nine people out of ten. Every now and again the calls rang out from close at hand, and were answered from somewhere in front.

He felt sure that their approach was being signalled from sentry to sentry as they drew near to the outlaw's hiding-place. His heart beat faster as he thought that in a few moments he might be face to face with the notorious leader himself.

There was wood-smoke in the air. He sniffed. It was like the smell of the village, when every fire was alight. For an instant he felt homesick, but he choked down the feeling.

He had finished with home, ploughing the lord's fields, toiling and slaving under the bailiff's whip.

For the future he was an outlaw, a masterless man. His blood raced at the thought. Then suddenly, before he had time to realize it, they were standing in the midst of the outlaw village.

Village, he called it in his mind, for it was not a camp, but it was quite unlike Oxton or any other village he had ever seen.

It was a dell, sheltered on one side by a sandstone cliff, in the face of which were several caves. Close by, in a scattered semicircle, were half a dozen log huts, their sides thickly daubed with mud and over-grown with creepers and briars. There was a tiny plot of cultivated ground, but none of the wide fields which surrounded his own home.

'We don't go in for farming much,' said his guide with a laugh. 'There's always the chance we may have to move in a hurry, before the seeds come up.'

They advanced towards the caves. One or two men were standing about and called out to Dickon's companion. Some ragged-looking women, who were bent over fires cooking, or kneeling to wash clothes in a stream, glanced up curiously and then went on with their work. There were one or two small children who stopped their game to stare.

'Here we are,' said the outlaw, leading the way into the largest cave. It narrowed into a passage, twisted, and widened again into a spacious cavern, with other passages opening out beyond.

Light streamed in through a hole in the roof. The floor was dry and sandy, and mostly covered with deer-skins. Great antlers and boar-tusks adorned the walls.

A man and woman rose from their stools on either side of a roughly-made hearth.

'I've brought a recruit, Robin,' said Dickon's guide.

'Have you, Alan?'

Robin Hood came forward and clapped his hands on the boy's shoulders with a friendly gesture. The keen blue eyes were like steel, searching his face.

At first glimpse of the outlaw leader, Dickon had felt a sensation of disappointment.

He was quite old. If his sharp beard had been black instead of foxy-gold, it would have greyed by now. He did not look the wonderful hero of whom the songs and stories told.

When he met those steel-blue eyes, and felt the hands, friendly but strong, gripping his shoulders, he knew differently. This was a man among men.

He might be affable and pleasant, not haughty like a baron, but he was something bigger and stronger than any of the men who went with rich armour and gay banners, and made working men kneel as they passed.

'So you want to be one of our little band, eh?' He laughed musically, deep in his chest. 'Think it's a fine life, I suppose, eating the King's venison and the lord's mutton? It's not all May games, my lad. You'd be better at the plough in your own village.'

'I don't think so, sir,' said Dickon with a smile.

'There aren't many outlaws live to be as old as I am,' Robin warned him. 'They may sing fine ballads about us in the villages and towns, but they forget the rough parts. Nights out in the rain, every man trying to slit our throats, hunger and danger –'

'We get hungry in the villages,' said Dickon quietly. 'Besides, sir, I've no choice. I shot a hart two nights ago.'

'Did you? A hart? Not bad for a boy, eh, Alan? A cool hand to be picking off the King's harts at his age! How old are you?'

'Sixteen, sir.'

'All right, don't call me "sir". We're comrades in Sherwood, all equal. What's the sense of getting rid of one master and taking a new one?'

'Come and have some dinner, all of you,' said the woman from the fireside. 'I expect you and the boy are hungry, Alan.'

'Well, I am,' they both said together, and everyone laughed.

'I expect Alan's got some good things in that bag,' said Robin, and they all sat down on the stools.

Dickon ate ravenously. Not only was it his first proper meal for a day and a half, but it was the best he had ever eaten in his young life.

There was broth, full of meat as well as barley and vegetables, and fish (which he had hardly ever tasted before – it went to the castle and the monasteries), and creamy cheeses, and fruit.

'Don't think we always fare as well as this,' said Robin. 'We've been doing well lately, that's all.'

After the meal, they went outside to test Dickon's shooting. Robin had already questioned him carefully on all he could do, until the boy almost began to imagine that he would be an important addition to the band.

'I like to know what people can do – and what they can't do,' explained the outlaw. 'Then I can depend on them in an emergency.'

'Could you hit the white spot, do you think?' asked Alan-a-Dale doubtfully.

This was the harder kind of target. The easier was a clout, a white cloth stretched on a hoop.

'I'd like to try.'

They set up the target and several outlaws gathered to watch. Dickon aimed five shafts from the usual distance, and three of them found the mark.

'Good for a boy!' shouted someone.

'And excellent for a villager,' said Alan with a grin. 'Practice makes perfect. Make up your mind to get five out of five next week.'

'I will,' vowed Dickon happily.

He kept his word. The outlaws welcomed him readily to their band and he was given a sleeping-place in Alan's hut. For ten days he did nothing but odd jobs of one kind and another, and had plenty of time to practise archery. At the end of a week he was able to plant his five arrows truly in the mark.

Days passed. It was pleasant not to have to work so hard as at home, but life was not very exciting, and again he felt a slight feeling of disappointment.

Outlaws came and went on mysterious missions. Sometimes Robin himself went off with a dozen of them, but he was never asked to accompany them. He felt out of it, and wondered whether they doubted him still.

At last came the day when Robin beckoned him into his own cave. 'I've got a job for you, my lad.'

Dickon followed eagerly.

'I want you to go to Nottingham. Do you think you could manage it?'

'In disguise?' asked the boy breathlessly.

'Well, if you go in Lincoln green they'd string you up from the nearest beam,' said the outlaw with a laugh. 'You must put on some clothes I've got here and call yourself an apprentice. Yes, a weaver's apprentice, because it's to a weaver you're going.'

'What shall I call myself?'

'What you like. You're from Mansfield, your master is Nicholas Fletcher, and you're carrying a message from him to Master Thomas Pole of Nottingham, whose sign you will find in Goose Gate.'

Robin picked up a package and balanced it on his hand.

'There is the message. Don't trouble to hide it, for it reads quite innocently to anyone but Master Pole. Get it to him if you can, though, and do as he says.'

'I see,' said Dickon, his eyes shining. 'And when shall I see you and the others again?'

Robin smiled at his excitement and stroked his beard slowly.

'If all goes well, in Nottingham marketplace!'

Chapter Four

Into the Lion's Mouth

Dickon caught his first glimpse of the town from Gallow's Hill. He had passed, with a shudder, the swinging corpses, tarred to preserve them longer, which gave the hill its grisly name. Now, as he tramped the last straight mile of the Mansfield road, he saw the crowded roofs of Nottingham below.

There were two towns really, clustered on opposite hills, with an open space between them. On the eastward hill loomed the great mass of St Mary's Church, and the houses of the Saxons seemed to nestle as close under its shadow as they could. To the west rose the steep sandstone rock on which the Conqueror had planted one of his chief fortresses, and at its foot the Norman town had gradually sprung up. There were still times when a Norman was unsafe in the Saxon quarter.

It was the huge castle which held Dickon's gaze, and caused him to shiver more than the creaking gibbet had done. He was getting used to death beside the highway. But this frowning stronghold on the cliff was something different.

It straddled across the road from north to south. With its twin-fortress at Newark, it commanded the two main crossings of the River Trent, and he who held both could cut England in two. Like some evil vampire, it crouched on its rock, sucking the blood from the countryside. On every side but one the rock was almost sheer, and not a man, let alone an army, could scale it. The one thin tongue of passable ground was defended by moats and drawbridges and round towers of immense strength.

Men talked, sometimes, in whispers of the day when the castle would fall, when its dungeons would open and let out the blind, tortured wretches who languished there. But they spoke of it hopelessly, as if they were speaking about the end of the world.

If ever the castle fell, it would be the end of the world, the old world of torture and tyranny....

Meanwhile Dickon approached the town.

He could not restrain a feeling of excitement as he drew near. He had never been to Nottingham before, though he had heard of its wonders, and, despite the danger of his mission, he was determined to enjoy himself.

At the same time there might be, among all the strange faces of the townsfolk, someone who recognized him as the runaway boy from Oxton, and who would raise the hue and cry.

They had done their best to disguise him. He had put on a suit such as apprentices wore and looked a proper young townsman. He had combed his hair for once, and that alone would have baffled anyone used to seeing tousle-headed Dickon in the old days. Robin had taught him a few things to say if anyone questioned him about weaving or his master.

There were plenty of other people entering the town, and he passed under the forbidding archway without challenge. Once in the cobbled streets he breathed a sigh of relief. It was impossible that

anyone should recognize him among such a pack
of folk.

At first he was quite bewildered. He stumbled
along the narrow thoroughfare all eyes and ears for
the strange sights and sounds about him. After he
had bumped into several men and been heartily
sworn at, and had tripped over a dog and fallen into
a patch of horse-muck, he began to look where he
was going. On both sides of the street were open
shops and booths, with boys like himself shouting
one against the other, as if they possessed lungs of
brass. Dickon paused to look at one who was holding
up steaming hot ribs of beef on a platter.

'What d'ye lack?' sang the apprentice, thrusting
the meat under his nose.

'Eh?' stammered Dickon.

'What d'ye lack?' bellowed the youth.

'Er – nothing. Thanks.'

'Anyone with half an eye can see you couldn't
afford beef, anyhow,' retorted his questioner rudely.

Dickon flushed and clenched his fists. Then he
grinned sheepishly and went on his way. It would
never do to get into a fight, and perhaps arrested,
before his precious message was delivered.

It was fatal to stand still for a moment. He was
sure to be surrounded by noisy, blustering lads, all
trying to sell him something. He had never heard
such a row in his life. They were like a lot of terriers.

At length he reached Weekday Cross, the open
space on the hillside below the church, where every
day hawkers and merchants, cheapjacks and peasants, gathered to sell their wares and shout one
against the other. Close by was Goose Gate, and in a

few moments he found himself at the house of
Master Thomas Pole, the weaver.

'So you've brought me a message from Nick
Fletcher, have you?'

The weaver was a fat, jolly sort of man, and he
winked as he greeted Dickon. He led the way into a
room at the back of the house and produced a flagon
of wine.

'Old enough for wine, eh?' he asked with a grin.

'You bet!'

The boy drained the sharp red liquid, trying not
to make a face at its bitterness. A delicious warm
glow spread through his body.

'I reckon you don't taste much o' that in
Sherwood – in Mansfield, I mean.' The weaver cor-
rected himself with another smile. 'Have a piece o'
this, too. There's not many in Nottingham live as

well as we do. Not that we couldn't do with a bit more, all the same.'

Dickon produced the letter from his wallet and his host smoothed it out on the table. He read it slowly, his bushy eyebrows knitted, his long forefinger spelling out the words. Dickon, who could not read, watched and wondered how these black scrawls and lines could possibly carry Robin's words to the weaver.

'No one else seen this?' said Master Pole quickly, when at last he had mastered the message and stowed it away in his own wallet.

'No one.'

'Right. Do you know what it's all about?'

'Only a bit. There's going to be a riot, isn't there?'

Master Pole laughed.

'If it's a riot, it will be the fault of the Sheriff, not us. The honest tradesmen and workmen of the town are going to hold a meeting. We have complaints to make. And above all we want to release some of our neighbours whom the Sheriff has clapped into jail –'

'Into the Castle?' interrupted the boy breathlessly.

'Oh no. We'd never get them out of there. They're in the town jail – for nothing at all but daring to speak their minds'

'And we're going to set them free?'

'Oh no!' Master Pole gave one of his winks. 'But we shall ask the dear kind Sheriff to let them go. And perhaps when he sees us all in front of his house, some of us with hammers and hatchets we forgot to leave at home –'

'He'll give in?'

'Perhaps. And perhaps not. More likely he'll order out his men.'

'And then?'

'If Robin Hood has come to town, they may get more than they bargained for.'

That night Dickon went to a meeting with the weaver, who had promised him lodging until the day. The meeting was secret. It was held in the sandstone caves and passages which, like the catacombs of Rome, wound hither and thither under the town.

Master Pole's own cellars were only caves, smoothed in places, levelled and fitted with doors and steps. By the light of a torch the weaver led him into the farthest corner, pulled aside some casks, and revealed an opening beyond.

'This is my back door,' he chuckled. 'Very useful, at times.'

Dickon kept close behind him, watching the ground at his feet for sudden chasms. It was very weird, this journey through the bowels of the earth. Strange to think that above him, through yards of solid brown rock and earth, people were treading the streets under the moon.

How did the weaver find his way? To Dickon the place seemed like a honeycomb. Fresh passages and caves opened out every few yards, but his guide strode on without faltering, never taking the wrong turning, never even hesitating for an instant.

'Is it much farther?' whispered the boy. He hated this feeling of being trapped like a rat in a hole. He would have given anything to have seen the tree-tops and stars over his head again.

'Here we are.' They stepped, blinking, into a large cavern, the roof of which soared upwards out of sight. Some twenty men were gathered there and almost as many torches were stuck in crevices to light up the scene.

Thomas Pole read Robin's letter to the meeting and after that Dickon scarcely understood half of what was said. The men talked quickly and angrily, sometimes interrupting one another, sometimes almost quarrelling. He heard the King spoken of in a way he had never heard before, even among the outlaws, and at first, because he had been brought up to revere him, he felt slightly shocked. Soon he realized that it was true what these men were saying, that the King and the barons were equally useless to the people. If they could be got rid of, with their wars and taxes and selfish sport, everyone would be far better off.

CHAPTER FOUR

Dickon had always thought that townsfolk had a better time than people in the country, but he learnt now that there was not much to choose between them. If the merchant or craftsman handled more money than the peasant, he was only asked to give more to the King.

He had always thought, too, that it was the fault of the Normans. He found out now that there were poor Normans, just as there were rich Saxons. It was wealth and power, not name, that mattered.

'Don't you see?' said a swarthy bridle-smith. 'We'll never end our troubles till all of us unite against the barons. They fool us, setting one lot against the other lot, and while we're scrapping among ourselves, they sit in their castles laughing at us. It isn't Normans against Saxons, it's masters against men.'

'Yes,' said Pole nodding. 'It's a cunning trick of theirs.'

'An old one,' put in a young scholar from Oxford. 'Divide et impera.'

'What the devil's that?' growled the bridle-smith.

'It means "divide – and rule",' said the scholar proudly. 'It's Latin.'

'Latin won't solve our troubles – or open the door of the jail. Now we've got to plan....'

Heads drew closer together and voices were lowered until Dickon, nodding sleepily on a smooth shelf of rock, could no longer catch what was being said.

Slowly the torches guttered out with a splutter and a cloud of black smoke. The meeting went on, heedless of the gathering darkness.

Tired by his long journey and the excitements of the town, Dickon fell asleep.

Chapter Five

The People Speak

Across the vast market-place of Nottingham ran a wall, built to divide the Norman quarter from the Saxon. But today no one could see the wall except those who were tight pressed against it. On both sides an angry crowd surged slowly backwards and forwards, eddying and murmuring.

Pale faces, some frightened, some curious and eager, peered from the windows and galleries of Long Row, Angel Row, and the other houses overlooking the square.

A little farther away, a little apart, the Castle and its crag seemed to block the whole western sky. Its haughty banner flapped darkly, like the wing of some evil bird of prey, hovering over the town. But no one was bothering about the Castle today.

'One – two – three!' chanted the burly bridlesmith standing on the top of the market wall. Thousands of voices took up the cry together.

'We – want – the Sheriff!'

Dickon had become separated from his friend the weaver, and had wormed his way through the crowd until he was near the centre. In one hand he clutched a staff, while the other fingered the handle of his hunting-knife. He could see that most of his neighbours were armed in one way or another; butchers had brought their knives and smiths their hammers.

Everyone had at least a cudgel. There was trouble brewing.

'We – want – the Sheriff!' rose the shout again.

Dickon had not recognized a face from Sherwood, but he knew that they were all about him, disguised in the dust and rags of pedlars and pilgrims. When the signal was given, bows would appear from nowhere, and the King's men would fall as freely as the King's deer.

Hardly had the last word of that tremendous roar died away than a sudden hush fell on the throng. Like a forest fire, the news sprang from lip to lip. The Sheriff was coming!

Dickon stood on tiptoe and craned his neck.

A double rank of pikemen was advancing slowly through the crowd on the Norman side of the wall. Sullenly the people gave back. Those who were nearest the pikemen were in no hurry to feel the sharp points between their ribs.

'Halt!' barked a voice. The two ranks turned, stepped back, and crossed their pikes, leaving a clear avenue fenced with two lines of steel. Down it rode the Sheriff.

He drew rein at the wall and stared at the bridle-smith on the top of it. Words passed between them, but few could catch what they were.

Suddenly the smith turned and cried to the waiting throng: 'Friends!'

There was a roar of encouragement. When it died away, he went on quickly:

'Neighbours, whoever you are, Normans or Saxons –'

Once more the vast crowd shouted its agreement.

'Our lords and masters will not listen to our demands! So the poor may go hungry while the rich eat themselves sick – and honest men may go to jail for saying so –'

The two nearest pikemen, at a signal from the Sheriff, lunged at him, but he hopped nimbly away. There was a rush of pikemen towards him, and he waited only to utter one last shout before leaping down into safety among the people.

'To the jail, my hearties!'

To the jail!

Suddenly everyone was shouting again as though he were mad. There was a great surge forward, which carried Dickon along with it, as helpless as a twig in a rushing stream. Sticks and other weapons were brandished overhead.

Then the crowd surged back again, and Dickon with them, the breath almost choked out of his body.

I didn't know fighting was like this, he thought ruefully to himself. I can't draw my knife, I can't lift my stick, and I can't even see the enemy. I'm packed as tight as a fish in a barrel.

After a minute or two he was able to scramble on to the wall and see what was happening.

Slowly, fighting step by step, the people were giving back before the remorseless spear-points of the Sheriff's men. Wool jersey and leather apron could not stand against such weapons, and sticks could make no impression on mail coats and steel helmets. Growling like a wounded animal, the crowd walked backwards before that unbroken line.

Part of the square was already cleared, except for a body here and there, or a wounded man crawling away with shattered collarbone or bleeding limb. The Sheriff rode backwards and forwards behind his men, hounding them on to further efforts.

'Whip them home to their kennels, the puppies!' He twirled his moustaches angrily – and at that moment an egg shattered itself on the nosepiece of his helmet, and spread over most of his face. 'Get the man who threw that!' he screamed. 'I'll have him dancing on air tonight!'

Where was Robin Hood?

Anxious looks were turning every way. He had promised his help, and in a few minutes it would be too late. The crowd would be pushed back into the narrow streets and broken up.

Suddenly a horn rang out. Dickon's heart jumped. He knew that note.

Sixty men leapt on to the wall. They looked like honest country people come to market – one or two, even, wore the skirts and shawls of peasant women – but in every left hand was a six-foot bow, in every right hand a cloth-yard arrow. In a second, every bow was bent, a goose-feather tip drawn to each outlaw's ear.

The crowd had slipped back a little, leaving a clear space in front of the stupefied pikemen. It was safe to shoot.

'Let us pass in peace,' came the high, bell-like voice of Robin Hood. 'Otherwise–'

'Charge!' snarled the Sheriff, urging his horse forward.

'Shoot!' retorted the outlaw.

Sixty shafts gleamed for a moment in the sunshine. They rattled on chain-mail and steel, but some pierced the links and others struck unprotected face and hand and leg. Several of the men-at-arms crashed forward on their faces. The whole line wavered, glaring nervously at the next flight of arrows ready on the string.

This was the bridle-smith's chance. 'To the jail, lads,' he yelled again, and once more the crowd swept forward.

The pikemen cowered before a second volley of shafts, and before they knew where they were, they were surrounded. Brawny hands wrenched their pikes from them, boys tripped them up, and others leapt on their backs from behind. There was no room to draw their swords. They were helpless and overpowered.

To the jail! Dickon was well to the fore in the race. They ran across the empty end of the square like a high tide. The Sheriff, still partly blinded by his egg, was pushed aside, his terrified horse rearing and threatening to bolt. His one concern for the present was to keep in the saddle.

Hatchets and crowbars were plentiful enough. It was the work of a minute to break down the door of the jail, and of another minute to bring out the prisoners, pale but smiling, into the open air. They were wise enough to make themselves scarce at once.

Not a moment too soon. The cry was raised: 'Horsemen from the Castle! Look out!'

From Friar Lane, the winding, rutted track which led from the market-place to the Castle, came the thunderous drumming of hoofs, the furious rattle of harness and arms.

'All right, lads. We've done what we wanted,' bellowed the bridle-smith. 'Home now. No sense in broken heads for nothing.'

'Back to Sherwood!' sang Robin somewhere near at hand.

Dickon ran with the rest. The horsemen charged in pursuit, lances levelled, long cruel swords swinging. The crowd melted like magic, vanishing into bystreets and alleys, dodging under the archways and the covered sidewalks, anywhere the riders could not follow them. Every now and again a goose-feathered shaft sped from behind a pillar, and a horseman crashed on the cobbles. The outlaws were doing their best to cover the retreat of the townsfolk.

One horseman made for Dickon, his long lance aimed at his heart. Dickon slipped under an overhanging gallery, but it was no use, the lance could reach him there. Out of the corner of his eye he saw a low archway leading into a lane. He ducked as the gleaming point came at him, slipped on the cobbles, and almost threw himself to safety. The man tried to follow, only to bump his head and wheel back, cursing, in search of easier prey.

Dickon found himself in a maze of empty streets where he had never been before. Blank houses, their few windows heavily shuttered, met his gaze. There was no one to ask the way to the North Gate, and he must get there without wasting a moment.

He ran round the corner, under another archway, found himself at a dead end, and tried again. Precious time was being wasted, time which might make all the difference between life and death.

Why hadn't he stuck to one of the other outlaws, to Alan or Much the Miller or Robin himself? He had been so anxious to be in the front of everything. He could have kicked himself for a young fool.

Ah, here was the street he remembered! Thank heaven, this would lead him to the gate.

He walked quickly, not daring to run. There were horsemen riding up and down now, questioning some people, seizing others. They must not notice him.

He turned the last corner. Hurrah! The gate was open.

Before his very eyes as he pressed forward it began to close. Too late, he broke into a run. He was still yards away when it clanged shut, and he realized he was trapped in the town.

At the same moment a horseman wheeled and stared him full in the face – the man from whom he had just escaped!

Chapter Six

In the Hands of the Enemy

One glance was enough for both man and boy.

With a yell, the rider dug his heels into the horse's flanks, but before the beast had recovered from its surprise, Dickon was haring back down the street. Close behind him came the clatter of hoofs, and the shouts of other men joining in the pursuit.

A low archway would not save him now. Head down, twisting and turning among the narrow lanes, he ran, expecting at any moment to feel the wind of the sword descending on his neck.

What chance had he, lost in an unknown town? Luckily, it was the Saxon quarter, and his pursuers had little more idea of the place than himself. Otherwise they would have caught him in a few moments.

A blind alley! And this time there was no chance to run back. The shouts were drawing nearer. He turned his back on the blank wall and drew his knife. At any rate he would make a fight for it.

Suddenly a casement shutter opened, high in the wall of a house at the side of the alley. A long wiry arm swung down towards him.

'Catch hold, and jump!' cried an urgent voice.

Without stopping to think, Dickon seized the offered hand and leapt. For a few horrid instants he swung, his legs scraping helplessly against the rough wall. He felt certain he was going to fall back into the arms of his enemies. But there was wonderful strength in the unknown's grasp. Dickon was pulled up and in. He fell forward on his hands in a dark room, and the casement slammed shut before the pursuers burst into the alley.

'Quick! They may search all the houses!'

Without wasting any more words, the man led him down a flight of stairs. Dickon found himself in a cellar very much like Master Pole's. Here, too, there was a concealed opening, leading on into natural caves.

'Follow the arrows,' said the man. 'They'll lead you to the caves on the far side of Gallow's Hill. Then you can find your way?'

'Yes, thank you.'

'Just mind, though – don't take any notice of the arrows unless they have a stroke scratched across them. If they haven't that, they're a blind to mislead our enemies.'

'I see.'

'Good luck.'

Clutching his torch, Dickon set off. It was easy enough, now he knew the trick of it. At frequent intervals were arrows cut in the soft rock, and most of them had a line through them. But every now and again the line was missing, and a plain arrow pointed the way to some dead end or wrong turning. Even if an enemy stumbled on the arrow clue, he would never notice the tiny difference between the signs, and would get lost, and even die for his pains.

People said that the first men of Nottingham, hundreds and thousands of years before, had lived in these caves. They were still used as cellars and store-rooms and (as Dickon now had cause to know) for other purposes too. The whole town was built on a vast underground maze.

He hoped the caves were not haunted by the men who had died there…. The very thought made him shudder. He stumbled on more quickly, anxious to reach the open air at the other end.

The passage had taken a turn downhill now. He felt his way cautiously, sliding his feet along the sandy floor, sometimes accidentally kicking a pebble which went bounding on into the darkness, awakening the echoes.

Suddenly, after a stone had bounced off his boot in this manner, he stopped short, stiffening with fear.

Instinctively his ears had waited for the sound of the pebble falling again – and no sound had come.

Then, after a pause, from a long, long way below him came a soft plop! as something struck water.

He swayed sickly for a moment, then had the presence of mind to drop to his knees and crawl forward, feeling every inch of the way. After a couple of yards the passage ended sharply in dank air and nothingness.

He lifted the torch and looked from side to side. Right across the floor yawned the gulf, and very far below he heard the sinister chuckle of lapping water.

Clearly, he had mistaken the arrows. He must have followed one without a stroke through it. How many intruders before him, he wondered, had made the same mistake, and now lay at the bottom of the abyss?

He must get back to the place where he had left

the right path. His torch was burning low, and the thought of being left in the dark was unbearable. He retraced his steps as quickly as he dared.

But it was no easy matter finding the arrows in the reverse direction. They had been scratched on the rock so as to guide men going from the town, and he had to keep looking back to find them. Haste was impossible.

'Out of the frying-pan into the fire,' he growled to himself.

It was good to think of frying-pans and the good supper there would be in Sherwood tonight. It helped to keep his courage up.

Here was a cave he could swear he had never passed before. He looked round desperately. Five passages led from it, and nowhere did the dying flame of his torch reveal an arrow, false or true.

'Better to have hanged than be buried alive,' he growled again. Grumbling was about all one could do under the circumstances.

He began to make his own marks with his knife, so that at least he should not try the same passages twice. Time after time he set out from the cave, only to return to it again. Was there no way from it?

There must be. He had got into it from the outside world. He could get back.

He remembered, with a sinking heart, that even if he found his way to the cellar again, the outlet was blocked by huge casks, which he could not possibly shift from the inside. He might knock and shout for days before anyone came down into the vaults and heard him.

Anyhow, he couldn't find the way back.... And the

torch was finishing.... Soon he wouldn't be able to see even his own knife-marks. How long did it take a man to starve to death?

The torch flared up in a last effort and burnt his fingers. He swore and dropped it. For a little while it lit up a circle of the sandy floor, then died to a red glow, and slowly faded out.

Leaving blackness.

Absolute blackness.

Dickon wondered whether to pray to the Saints to help him, as he had been taught. But he had given up praying to them long ago, because they never seemed much good. He had often prayed for food when his mother and all of them were starving, but the Saints had never been able to send as much as a crust. Saints were no use. No, if he ever got out alive, it would be by good luck and his own efforts.

What a tale to tell them all in Sherwood! If he ever got out....

Slowly and carefully, he groped his way along yet one more passage. His foot scrunched and snapped something which felt like the ribs of a skeleton.... Something round and heavy rolled aside, clattering. He clenched his teeth and went on.

For hours, it seemed, he stumbled through endless corridors and caverns. Sometimes he had to bend to avoid bumping his head, at others the roof of rock soared high beyond the tips of his upstretched fingers. Once he forded an underground stream, knee-deep and icy cold. He tried hopefully to follow it, knowing that sooner or later it must lead to open air, but it plunged almost immediately beneath a narrow arch of rock, leaving no more than an inch or two of space between. That way meant drowning.

He had left Nottingham in the afternoon. It must be night now, perhaps even another day. It seemed like a lifetime. He was so weary that he could have lain down and slept – if anyone could sleep in such a place of horrors.

On he crawled, drawing one cramped and dripping foot after the other. The gushing stream was left behind, and there was no sound but his own slow, dragging steps.

This was the end, surely. To die like a rat in a trap! Better almost to drive the knife into his own heart, and shorten the agony....

Then it was he saw the first gleam of pale, ghostly light.

Not really? Surely he was mistaken? He had so longed to see light, and now he was fancying it all.

But the light grew as he stumbled forward. A fresh current of warm air, fragrant with wild flowers, met him in the face. He could see bushes, and stars gleaming between the leaves.

Two minutes later he stood on the open hillside, drawing in great breaths of the evening air. The moon was rising over the high ridge of Mapperley, and a few hundred yards away the gibbets creaked beside the Mansfield road. With a sigh of relief he turned northwards towards Sherwood, whose line upon line of wooded hills lay friendly in the silver light.

For hours he tramped, almost sleeping as he walked, yet happy in the knowledge that every step took him farther from the perilous town. At last he caught the gleam of a fire and struck off the highway towards it.

All his fears and troubles were forgotten. How good it would be to hear a friendly voice again! How his heart had yearned for the comradeship of the greenwood!

'Hullo!' he called.

The men round the fire sprang up. Too late he recognized the livery of the King's foresters. He could have cried with disappointment and rage. However tired he was, he should have taken care.

'Who's this?' queried a sharp voice.

'Young Dickon of Oxton,' answered another. 'We want him.'

Before the boy could turn, he was seized roughly on all sides. Practised hands tied his wrists behind his back, and he was flung like a sack on to the wet ground.

This time he was properly in the hands of the enemy.

Chapter Seven

The Song of Freedom

Dawn broke soon afterwards. Weary and cramped, a mass of aches and pains, Dickon was dragged to his feet. To his great relief, however, the foresters were not going to Nottingham. They were making in the opposite direction.

There were six of them, sallow Gascons all of them, specially brought from the forests across the sea. They hardly understood the English speech, and they were not likely to show any favour to peasants. Dickon knew it would be useless to plead for mercy.

As they tramped along the highway, two of them kept arrows ever on the string, and eyed the undergrowth carefully on both sides. They knew of the riot which had taken place in Nottingham, and knew, too, that the forest was alive with fugitives.

It was a broad road, this main way to the North, and by law the bushes were cleared on either side to a considerable distance. There was no hope of a sudden ambush by Robin or any of his comrades.

In any case, thought Dickon dismally, they are probably miles away and have no idea what has happened to me. I am an expert at getting into trouble. If I ever get out of this, I'll have had enough adventures.

He had had nothing to eat since the day before. One of the foresters, kinder than the rest, gave him

a hunk of bread, and they all laughed to see him trying to eat it without the use of his hands. Eventually
half the bread fell into the road, and he nearly
choked with the great dry mouthful he had managed
to save. When they passed a stream they let him
kneel and lap what water he could.

Now the sun was mounting higher and there were
other people on the road. They stared curiously at
the foresters and the prisoner, some openly pitying
him, others making jokes, but most of them saying
nothing. It was not wise to show sympathy, but at any
rate they would not laugh.

Merchants passed, leading their strings of pack-
horses and donkeys, carrying bales of Beverley blue
and Stamford scarlet cloths, Sheffield knives, and
Cheshire salt, wool, salted haddocks, liquorice, and
a hundred and one other commodities.

Friars went by, and some stopped to patter a
prayer for the captive, as their founder, St Francis,
had told them. Dickon sniffed contemptuously. He
needed no praying over. He thought of how differently Friar Tuck would have behaved, that jovial outlaw who had left the Order in disgust and joined the
band. Tuck would have set about the foresters with
his great whirling quarter-staff.

There were pilgrims, too, weary-footed men and
women trudging uselessly from place to place in
order to be sure of going to Heaven when they got
tired of walking and died. Some were going north to
St Cuthbert's shrine at Durham, others south to
Canterbury, and a few meant to go right on to Rome
and Jerusalem.

'Ah, well, they see the country,' said one of the

foresters, 'and the people at Durham and Canterbury do well out of them.'

There were pedlars and beggars also on the road, ragged men who slunk by as if afraid of being stopped. On the crest of the hill they found one of these bedraggled creatures, squatting on the grass and tuning a small harp.

'Good morning,' he called in a shrill voice as they drew near. 'Who are you, slogging along like a company of soldiers?'

'The King's foresters. And who are you, Master Inquisitive?'

The harper looked blankly towards them, and they saw that he was blind. He chuckled and bent over his instrument again. 'Everyone knows me. I'm Hal the Harper. I've played before kings –'

'Well, play before us,' said the head forester good-humouredly. 'In front of us, I mean. We want something to march to.'

'If one of you will guide me!'

The player stood up and a Gascon took his arm. Something in his hunched-up figure and keen, bird-like face – half hidden though it was by dust and grime – struck Dickon as being familiar. Yet he could not recall having seen Hal the Harper before.

Certainly he was a wonderful player, and in the strains of his music the boy again thought he detected something he vaguely remembered. He groped in his mind to think where and when he had heard the tunes.

The blind man sang war songs of Normandy and love songs of Provence. He played Moorish music from Spain and deep melodies from Germany. He seemed to pluck magic from his strings, and the foresters could hardly help dancing in the roadway.

Then the harper began to sing in the broadest Nottinghamshire dialect, which hardly a Southern Englishman, let alone a Gascon, could understand. It was the speech of Dickon's own people, and he pricked up his ears.

'Take courage, lad,
and fear no harm,'

sang the harper suddenly. Dickon's heart leapt violently and he stared at the blind man trudging along beside him. But the man looked straight ahead, and surely it was only the boy's imagination that the nearer of those sightless eyes winked at him?

'No, do not stare at me.'

went on the singer,

'I'll tell you in my little song
How you will soon be free.'

Alan-a-Dale! Dickon could have shouted with relief. He listened intently for the next verse.

'These foreign fools don't understand
A word of what I sing,
So long as they can hear its rhyme,
Oh, ting-a-ling-a-ling!'

Dickon grinned. It must be hard making up poetry

and trying to think out plans at the same time. Alan
struck the harp again and carolled gaily.

'Walk slowly and pretend you're lame,
And that will give me time,
I'll go in front and make a plan –
Ti-tum-ti-tum I rhyme.'

'Ti-tum-ti!' laughed one of the foresters. 'What a daft language this English is!'

'Stow that song,' said the leader roughly. 'We've had enough of it. Sounds like nonsense to me.'

'I assure you,' said the harper bowing, 'it is full of meaning – very beautiful meaning.'

So it is, said Dickon to himself. But the foresters clamoured for another French song about girls, and they had to have their way.

At the next turning, Alan peered round blindly and asked: 'Is this where the road to Mansfield turns off? This is my way, masters.'

They gave him a coin and he hobbled gratefully away. The moment he was out of sight he straightened his back and began to run like a stag through the forest.

The foresters continued northwards with their prisoner. Remembering what he had been told, Dickon began to lag. His tiredness was not all put on, for he had had practically no sleep and was becoming exhausted. By pretending also to be lame, he contrived to waste a good deal of time during the next few miles. This would give Alan a chance to do something, though it was unlikely he could find enough outlaws to try an open attack on the foresters. Robin and the main body must be far in front by now.

Still, there was more than a ray of hope. The comrades never left one of their number to his fate. Boy as he was, Dickon had already become popular with them, and especially with Alan. Alan would find a way.

He was cunning as a fox. His disguise would have

taken in his dearest friend. Surely it was not beyond him to outwit six foresters? Things had not looked so hopeful for a long time.

'Hurry up, can't you?' said the head forester, sharply. 'There's a village we want to reach by noon. If you can get along faster, you shall have something to eat there.'

'I'm dead-beat,' muttered Dickon, dragging his feet in the dusty road.

'Come along!' And they lugged him forward by the elbows.

On they went under the torrid sun. After a time one of the men looked around and exclaimed: 'There's a lot of horsemen coming up behind. Must be a hundred.'

Everyone looked back.

'It's the D'Eyncourt livery,' said another. 'Maybe it's Sir Rolf come back from the Crusade.'

'It is,' answered the head forester slowly. 'A hundred, eh? And they reckon he took three hundred out with him.'

Dickon's heart thumped wildly. His own father must be in this cavalcade which was rapidly approaching. All thought of his own plight was forgotten in the hope of seeing his father again.

The horsemen drew near. That was Sir Rolf in front, in the yellow surcoat with the crimson eagle – 'blood and jaundice' men called his colours, and his temper, they added, was tinged with the same hues. But at the moment his sallow face was smiling under his lifted visor, and his yellow horse-teeth were bared in a grin as he listened to the man riding at his side.

The foresters and their prisoner drew into the

side of the road and stood respectfully for the column to pass. As Sir Rolf drew level, Dickon saw to his alarm that his companion was Master William, the bailiff, who must have ridden out to meet his lord. At that moment the bailiff chanced to look down and his fat face lit up.

He whispered something quickly to Sir Rolf. The knight raised his arm as a signal and the whole column reined up.

'Forester,' he said leaning forward, 'is that one of my serfs you have there?'

'Yes, Sir Rolf. Dickon of Oxton, sir.'

'Well, he's a runaway.' The knight scowled and gave an ugly snarl. 'I want him. I'll deal with him.'

'But, sir –'

'He'll be safer in a dungeon of D'Eyncourt Castle. He won't break forest laws again.'

Dickon listened horrified. This meant goodbye to any plan Alan might make. This time he was surely done for.

Friends in Need

Sir Rolf leered down at the head forester, but the man gave him stare for stare. Dickon stood miserable, waiting for his fate to be decided.

Once inside D'Eyncourt Castle, he could give up all hope. Sir Rolf had a way of dealing with runaway serfs... to discourage others. All the outlaws in Sherwood would hardly get him out again, once he had passed that drawbridge and the portcullis had rattled down behind him.

'I'm sorry, sir,' said the forester. 'He must answer to forest law, first. Afterwards –'

'But I tell you –' blustered the knight.

The forester stood his ground. There were not many men who dared to argue with Sir Rolf. For the first time, Dickon began to like the forester.

'I'm the King's man. And the King's justice must be done first.'

'What if I take him?'

The knight glanced meaningly to his men, the nearest of whom were listening eagerly to the conversation. Their eyes brightened at the prospect of a brush with the foresters, for there was no love lost between the two bodies of men.

The half-dozen archers would be ridden down in a moment by these full-armoured horsemen. Surely they would not attempt to defy Sir Rolf any longer?

'I'm the King's man,' repeated the forester stolidly. 'I'm sorry, sir, but if you interfere with me in my duty, it will be – rebellion. You will have to answer for that to the King.'

'All right, all right.' Sir Rolf swore with annoyance. 'You can argue like a lawyer, my man. Take the boy, for the present, but let me have him back – when you've done with him. And mind he's not spoilt for work. Hard work.'

'He will be tried and punished by the forest court,' said the man smoothly. 'Good day, sir.'

'Good day!' And muttering to himself the knight urged his horse forward, and the whole column jerked into life behind him.

Almost overcome with relief though he was, Dickon had not forgotten his father, and, as the long cavalcade trotted past, he searched the ranks for his face.

It was no good. Many faces he recognized, men from his village, tanned by southern heat and slashed with scars, but there were many remembered features missing, and among them his father's. As the last rank went by he could no longer contain himself, and called out to a man he knew. The rider looked back, his hard face softened into sympathy.

'Dead,' he flung back. 'He was killed at –'

The end of his sentence was lost in the dust and distance as the column clattered on.

Dickon blinked back a few tears as he walked on with his captors. Just one more score to settle with his masters, if ever he got free again!

Now they were descending a long slope to where the roofs and smoke of a small village showed above the tops of the trees. The foresters began to smack their lips loudly at the thought of drink.

Nor was it only a thought for long. Within five minutes they were sitting on wooden benches outside the ale-house, and their host was measuring out the pewter tankards. Several other villagers gathered round to stare, and there were many glances of sympathy for Dickon, and dislike for the foresters.

The boy's hands were freed for a while, and he was allowed to buy himself food and drink, which he swallowed eagerly after his long fast. Besides, if there was going to be a chance of escape, he must keep his strength up.

'Aren't you ashamed of yourselves, doing the dirty work for our masters?'

At this sudden question the foresters looked up in surprise. The speaker was the village smith, a muscular, red-faced man who had stepped across from his forge, hammer in hand.

'What do you mean?' said the head forester.

'Well, you and me's common folk, aren't we?'

'I'm the King's forester –'

'That makes no difference. We both work – and hard – just so as our master can sit at ease.'

'That sounds like treason, my man.'

'It's sense.' There were murmurs of approval from the other villagers, who were increasing in number as more and more came to see what was happening. 'Common sense,' repeated the smith. 'I reckon we all ought to stand in together against the men on top. And to begin with, you ought to let the lad go. He's one of us.'

'Don't be a fool.' The head forester got to his

feet. He did not like the look of this crowd which was closing in upon him. 'Let's have no more of that talk, and think yourself lucky I don't arrest you –'

'Lucky!' The smith flung back his great head and roared with laughter. 'Think yourself lucky you haven't tried, Frenchy.' He slapped his thigh with a hand which might have felled an ox.

There were louder murmurs among the crowd, laughter at the foresters, sympathy with the captive, and an increasing anger. Dickon searched their friendly faces anxiously, but there was none he could recognize. Stay! Was it fancy again or was that the blind harper stealing round the back of the group, whispering a word here, giving a nudge there?

'Drink up, boys,' said the forester quickly. 'We'll be getting on, now. Tie his hands again.'

'Hanged if they do!' bellowed the blacksmith. 'What about it, neighbours? Are we going to stand by while –'

He stopped, his mouth open. Three arrows were pointing at his heart. Slowly and sullenly the crowd gave back.

Dickon saw his chance fading. In another moment his wrists would be tied again. It was up to him. He must take a risk and hope for the best.

He gathered his strength and leapt suddenly against the foresters who had drawn their bows. Like a shot at nine-pins, he cannoned from one to another, throwing all three off their balance. Two of the arrows sang harmlessly into the sky.

'Grab him!' yelled the leader.

Next moment he went down before the black-smith's fist. The village street was in an uproar.

Dickon's venture had not quite come off. He had taken his captors by surprise, but he had not got away. One of them held him now against the wall of the ale-house, a hunting knife at his throat. Dickon stood rigid and helpless, watching the fight from the corner of his eye.

Armed with any weapon which came to hand – hammers, pitchforks and the like – the villagers had sailed in with gusto. There was a long-standing feud between this place and the foresters, and it was a good opportunity to pay off old scores.

Though outnumbered, the foresters were much better armed. They had drawn their swords, having no chance to shoot, and formed a semicircle with their backs to the wall. Dickon and their unconscious leader were inside the ring.

Steel clanged on steel, and the sound mingled with the panting and shouting of both sides. Overhead hurtled stones and clods, hitting the villagers themselves almost as often as the foresters they were meant for. Even the women had come out to do their share, and that, perhaps, was why the missiles seldom landed where they were aimed. Dickon himself felt a clod break on his head, and was glad it had not been an egg. He could not help thinking of the Sheriff of Nottingham.

One of the foresters was down, his head cracked with a hammer, but their leader had revived and took his place.

'We must get into the inn and barricade it,' he cried to his men, and they began obediently to back towards the door.

Seeing its prey about to escape, the crowd redoubled its efforts, and for some time the foresters were too busy to do anything but defend themselves from the thrusting forks and other weapons which assailed them.

'Guy!' The head forester called urgently to the man who was guarding Dickon. 'Slit that cub's throat and come here and help.'

'Right.'

The man leered in the boy's face and held him powerless with his left hand. Dickon closed his eyes and waited, stiff with terror, for the stab of the dagger.

It was a long time coming.

Suddenly he realized that the grip on his shoulder had relaxed. He could no longer feel the man's rank breath in his face.

He opened his eyes, ready for any disappointment, prepared to find that the man was merely delaying matters to be cruel. But, even as it was, Guy the forester had delayed it too long.

He had slid quietly to the foot of the wall, and lay, staring upwards with dead, unseeing eyes, while a red patch gradually crept over the front of his jerkin.

Sword in hand, the blind harper was climbing through the window above him....

'Hurry up, Guy!' shouted the head forester over his shoulder.

'He's sending us instead!' sang Alan-a-Dale. He had thrust Guy's knife into Dickon's hand and together they flung themselves like tiger-cats upon the rear of the foresters.

After that, the fight was quickly over. The four foresters who could run did so – and with a speed which their own deer might have envied. The villagers hustled them out, sending a final volley of clods and horse manure to hasten them on their way. Their bows lay where they had dropped them, and there were no fears that they would try to return for them that day.

'Thanks, Alan,' panted Dickon gratefully.

'Thank these people,' laughed the outlaw. 'It was they who did it, today, not the bows and bills of Sherwood.'

'Ay, the people,' broke in the blacksmith. 'And if every man who used tools used them as we've done, there'd soon be an end of masters.'

'And an end of swords, too,' said a woman. 'It's the masters who make the wars, not we.'

Dickon thought suddenly of his father, and nodded. 'And now back to Sherwood,' cried Alan.

Chapter Nine

A Rescue Repaid

When he returned to the outlaw band, after his eventful week of absence, Dickon found its numbers swollen to nearly seventy, among whom he recognized some of the prisoners they had released from Nottingham jail. Not daring to rejoin their wives and families, these men had thrown in their lot with the outlaws until better times should come and they should be able to take up their old crafts and trades again.

It was a mixed gang, this little group of masterless men. Most of them were peasants like Dickon himself, but there was a sprinkling of ex-soldiers who had got tired of fighting wars for their lords; not a few craftsmen who had been forced to leave their own towns and could not get work elsewhere; a scholar who had fled from Oxford after killing a man; Friar Tuck, who had long given up preaching to people; and other odd characters.

Most of them hailed from the villages round Sherwood. A few had drifted south from Yorkshire, led by the fame of Robin Hood; one or two, like the good-natured giant, Little John, had come from the High Peak Forest of Derbyshire; and the old soldiers had come from no one knew where.

As for Robin, none knew whence he came. He was a mystery.

Some said he was of noble birth, an earl really, but when they said it in his hearing he would laugh deep in his foxy-gold beard.

'Aren't you satisfied with a common man as leader?' he would ask, growing serious suddenly. 'If you want to follow an earl, you can have your pick of them – but you won't go with me. Some fools no sooner lose one master than they look for another.'

Dickon never cared who Robin was, nor what he had been. It was what he said and did now that mattered. And the boy knew that he was a man for the people, against their oppressors.

July merged into golden August, and there was little work to do but the trapping of game, chopping firewood, and the everyday jobs of camp life. Sometimes they played games and had shooting matches. Sometimes Dickon strolled off by himself, or with another youth or two, and bathed in the Dover Beck or one of the other streams which ran through the forest. There was one fine place on the Dover Beck where the little river broadened out into a lakelet, shut in by pinewoods and a bracken-covered hill.

Once, after they had robbed some wealthy merchants – a job so easy that it wasn't worth reckoning as an adventure – Dickon was given ten silver pieces as his share of the spoil. He took five and paid a stealthy visit to his mother in the middle of the night, telling her to spend them slowly lest people should wonder where she got them.

It was a sultry evening in the middle of August when, with his particular friend Martin, a red-haired runaway apprentice from Barnsley, he discovered the

Fairy Pool, which was only a mile or so from the huts, and destined to become another favourite swimming-place.

Quickly they stripped off their Lincoln green and plunged into the sun-warmed waters, larking about and chasing one and another round and under a huge oak which had fallen down the bank. It was all so pleasant that they forgot the passing of time, till the growing chillness of the air made them notice that the sun had already disappeared.

'And we've nothing to dry on,' groaned Martin, 'we ought to have come out while there was still sunshine.'

They splashed dolefully towards the mossy bank where they had left their clothes.

'Good Lord!' exclaimed Dickon in horror.

'Our things!'

'They've gone!'

'Was this where we left them?'

Frantically, they searched every inch of the bank, nettling their bare legs considerably in the process. In vain. Suits, caps, bows, knives – all had vanished without a trace.

'Some silly fool playing a joke,' stormed Martin. 'Just wait till –'

Twang!

A three-foot arrow quivered in a tree-trunk within a few inches of his heart.

'Look out!'

Instinctively the two boys flung themselves into the undergrowth before a second shaft could fly with truer aim. Next moment it sang through the leaves above their heads.

'Forester!' hissed Dickon. 'Can't shoot for nuts!'

'Shut up! We must crawl away.'

Stung and scratched at every yard, they squirmed their way farther into the safety of the woodland. They could hear no sound of pursuit behind them. It was getting dusk and their unseen enemy had evidently no desire to risk a rough-and-tumble at close quarters. Still, he had their clothes and their weapons.

'It's no good,' said the apprentice mournfully. 'We shall have to go home like this.'

'Ow! It's agony.' Dickon stood up gingerly, rubbing his aching knees.

'It's freezingly cold too.'

They stood shivering in the gloom, their pale bodies criss-crossed with cuts and stings. The grass was dank with dew under their bare feet.

'We can't be seen like this,' moaned Dickon.

'We can't stay here all night,' retorted Martin more practically.

Slowly and gingerly, they picked their way homewards, halting at intervals to make sure that they were not being followed. Even in their own plight, they had sense enough to remember that they must not betray the headquarters of the band to any watching eyes.

When at last they saw the welcome gleam of the camp-fires in front, they tried to sneak unseen into their hut, but in vain. All the outlaws of the band seemed to be gathered round the fires or standing in the doorways – even Marian was laughing in the mouth of her cave – and the boys had to run a regular gauntlet. Their cheeks were scarlet when at last they vanished into their own hut and slammed the door. There, in two neat piles, were their clothes, with their bows and arrows on top.

Little John opened the door and put his jovial face round it.

'Perhaps that will teach you young fools,' he said, and there was a note of seriousness behind his joking manner. 'It might just as well have been a real forester –'

'He'd have shot a deal better!' retorted Dickon, licking his wounds.

'No doubt,' said Little John. 'Get into your clothes. We all march at midnight.'

March at midnight!

The boys forgot to be angry any more. Some excitement was afoot, and the thought of it set their blood racing through their chilled bodies. In a few moments they ran out to join the groups round the fires and ask them what it was all about.

Alan told them. 'Do you remember a little village, with an ale-house?' he said with a smile at Dickon. 'Where there's a big brawny blacksmith –'

'Yes, yes! Where they rescued me from the foresters.'

'Well, the foresters haven't forgotten.'

'They're going to punish the village?'

'Yes. A body of men is leaving Nottingham tonight. They'll arrive before dawn, before the men have scattered to the fields. They'll surprise the village, hang the smith, whip a dozen others, fine everybody more than they can pay –'

'Unless –' interrupted Dickon meaningly.

'Unless,' Alan agreed with a smile. 'As you know, we march at midnight.'

'How does Robin know about it?' asked Martin.

'A little bird,' laughed the harper. 'Little birds of the forest tell him everything – and little birds in the town too.'

'Well, we'll mop them up,' said Dickon confidently. 'How many of them are there?'

'Twenty to carry out the punishments.'

'Why, it'll be a walk-over!'

'And they're riding up with a hundred men bound for Yorkshire – just for company. And the hundred will wait to see the fun.'

'A hundred and twenty!' Dickon's face fell.

'Scared?' asked Martin.

'Scared yourself! It'll be fearfully – exciting.'

All the same, both boys had a somewhat empty feeling in their stomachs, which had nothing to do with food, when they lined up with the others that night. It was their first real fight, and neither was at all sure that he would like it very much.

In single file, with scarcely more noise than one man would have made, the seventy outlaws moved along the winding paths. Not a twig cracked, not a stalk snapped, as the chain of shadows snaked through the thickets. Even the boys had already learnt to walk so that hardly a bruised grass-blade would show where they had passed.

Robin's plan was to surprise the enemy on the road, at a spot two or three miles before they reached the village. If all went well, the revengeful officers would never get near that village. If they did, they would not find the men they wanted most, for a warning had been sent to the smith, and he would have taken to the woods with his friends long before the horsemen reached his forge.

'No one who helps us is ever allowed to suffer for it – if we can help it,' Alan explained. 'That's why we have more and more friends among the villages.'

There was no more talking now. Like phantoms they glided on their way. There was no naked metal to catch the moonlight trickling through the leaves. The cloth of Lincoln green shrouded everything, even their sword-scabbards.

It was moon-set when they reached the appointed spot, a dip in the road where a shallow brook ran right across, its firm pebbly bed making a ford. This stream ran through a spinney of brambles and low trees, which crept right up to the roadway on either side, and had not been cleared as the undergrowth usually was.

The outlaws were thus able to shoot from close range and in perfect concealment, while the boggy ground through which the brook wound its way would be a serious hindrance to horses. It was an ideal place for an ambush.

Robin posted fifty men in the spinney, half on one side of the road, half on the other. Dickon and Martin went with Alan on the right hand. Ten men were posted well behind, to pick off any horsemen who burst through, while the remainder concealed themselves far in front, with instructions to lie low until the enemy were in retreat, and then hasten their departure.

The orders were simple. Shoot on the sound of the bugle. So far as was possible, pick out the officers of the law, and aim at the soldiers only in self-defence. If it was light enough, their colours would show the difference.

An hour of waiting followed, a long chilly hour, in which Dickon felt almost as cold and miserable as during his escapade earlier in the night. Dawn was coming slowly, a pale grey light. There was no sound but the gurgling of the stream.

Then, at long last, the far-off tramp of hoofs, the clink-clink of harness!

Dickon watched Alan like a cat, and imitated him exactly. Without a sound, he strung his bow, fitted a shaft to the string, and waited. Half a dozen other arrows were stuck in the ground in front of him, ready to snatch.

The first horsemen splashed through the stream. Alan raised his bow and drew back the goose-feather arrow-tip to his ear. Dickon did the same....

He must decide whom to aim at. His arrowhead swung from side to side as he made up his mind.

Ha-haaa! shrilled the silver bugle.

Like the swish of an April shower fifty shafts fell on the column of riders, pattering on chain-mail, piercing flesh and cloth.

Men and horses tumbled confusedly in heaps. Beasts reared, dazed troopers scrambled to their feet. The air was full of shouts and thuds.

Ha-haa! It was a trumpet this time, a signal to the soldiers. They wheeled outwards into two lines and at a second call charged, left and right, into the spinney.

'Shoot – for your life!' grunted Alan.

His own fingers positively twinkled as he picked up arrows and shot them into the struggling mass. Instinctively, Dickon followed suit. There was no time to aim properly, no time to distinguish between two sorts of enemy. Wherever he saw the glint of armour or heard the crackling of undergrowth he loosed a shaft in that direction.

A huge shadow loomed up ten yards away, horse and rider black against the dawn light, and a long sword that gleamed and flashed....

Crash! Smash! Crackle!

More of the great war-horses flung themselves against the undergrowth, trampling it down. The arrows sped silently amid the general uproar. A dappled grey suddenly fell clean through the last barrier of brambles and rolled kicking at Dickon's feet. Next moment, to his alarm, its rider followed, but unhurt and brandishing his sword.

No time for an arrow. The boy whipped out his own weapon and dodged behind a tree. Where were Alan and Martin and the others? He seemed to be alone in the wood with a six-foot man-at-arms, protected by close-linked mail, and twice as strong as himself.

Dickon lashed out wildly. The man countered easily, and leapt forward to press his advantage.

That leap, which should have finished Dickon, was the man's undoing. He slipped on the soaking grass and rolled over into the stream. There he struggled for a time, too heavily burdened by his armour to get up, and Dickon could easily have jumped down and finished him. But killing in cold blood made no appeal to him, and in any case there were more pressing matters demanding his attention. He saw the man no more.

Martin was struggling with another dismounted man, who was, luckily, wounded in his right shoulder and so unable to wield his sword at full strength. Dickon leapt to the rescue with a shout, and brought his own sword down on the man's helmet. He fell, and Dickon, knowing that Martin could manage now, picked up his bow again.

There was no need for it. The wood was empty and silent, except for a groaning man here and there. He ran after the others to the roadside, and was just in time to see the tail-end of the column riding furiously back to Nottingham.

Apart from a few sword-cuts, there were no casualties on the outlaws' side, for only a handful of the riders had ever come within striking distance. They on their part had suffered heavily, and the road was littered with the traces of the encounter.

Under Robin's instructions the outlaws gathered up all the weapons and armour. Many looked surprised, for it had never been done before. The outlaws relied on bows, short swords, and long bills like pole-axes. They had no use for lances and mail.

'We may need them – some day,' said Robin thoughtfully, and Alan nodded as if he, at least, knew when.

'Take these to our friend the smith,' went on the outlaw leader, telling off a party of men and pointing to a heap of the collected weapons. 'Tell him to hide them till the day. Till the day.' Robin smiled at his own secret thoughts. 'And tell him that no harm shall come to the village so long as we can hold the road.'

Chapter Ten

The Mailed Fist

Over the tall, square keep of D'Eyncourt Castle floated the banner which indicated Sir Rolf's return from the Holy Land. A spread eagle, blood-crimson on a golden field, it flapped in the summer breeze like the sinister bird of prey it represented.

The Eagle of D'Eyncourt had come home.

Perched on the body of the land, red claws sunk deep in the flesh of the peasantry, it drank the very life-blood of the surrounding country.

Sir Rolf had brought many things back with him besides the faked relics he had purchased to put in his chapel. He had brought new notions of luxury and cruelty, learnt in the rotting courts of Eastern Europe. And for these he must have more wealth and power, ever more wealth and power.

Those of his tenants who, fretting under the harsh yoke of his bailiff, had hoped for better times now that the lord himself was home, were sadly disappointed with what they found.

He looked out of the narrow window-slits of his stronghold and saw the land that was his, all his, stretching away in cornland and pasture, orchard and trout stream, to the confines of the King's forest. Out of this, and this alone, must his riches come.

For his feasting and drunkenness, the men must sweat and groan with plough and spade.

For his music must the tiny children spend all day alone, scaring crows or minding pigs.

For his clothes of rich cramoisy and samite must the village women crawl ragged and shivering through the winter.

For his pride must the best horses, the tallest men, the cleverest boys, waste their time dashing hither and thither to attend him.

'Well,' he would have bellowed at anyone who questioned him, 'it's all mine, isn't it?'

He must have more. They must drive the plough faster, glean more carefully, stuff his barns fuller. What if they fainted at their work? There was the whip, wasn't there, to revive them?

Minstrels and story-tellers, with a watchful eye on his temper and his boot, chanted in his hall wonderful stories about knights who helped the weak. Priests talked of the ideals of chivalry, and how wonderful it was to be a great and good man – like their master. Sir Rolf clapped the minstrels and hiccupped a hearty 'Amen' to the priests. Then he sent for his bailiff and told him to screw more work out of his tenants.

The mailed fist... the iron screw....

Between them they brought sorrow that summer to every family on the great D'Eyncourt estate.

Runaway serfs took the news to the outlaws. Tales of whippings and fines; of blows and kicks; of forced labour and longer hours on the lord's fields.

Robin listened with a grave face, stroking his golden beard in thought. 'Why don't the people turn on them?' growled Little John. 'I wouldn't stand it.'

'No, you wouldn't,' laughed Robin. 'But we're not all seven-foot giants with fists like hammers. What chance have these poor devils with their scythes and forks against men in mail, and on horseback?'

'Can't we help?' put in Dickon anxiously. He was thinking of his own village of Oxton, and the news that had come yesterday of fresh orders from Sir Rolf, meaning more work, more than the villagers could ever do.

'We must talk it over, all of us. We'll have a council tonight, and our friend here can tell his story to everyone.'

That evening there were close upon a hundred men gathered round the big central fire after supper. One of the runaways got up and described the harsh conditions under which the peasants were working, and there were growls of sympathy and agreement.

'We can't all run to the forest,' concluded the serf. 'We have our families to think of. And how could Sherwood feed such a multitude? We can only live on the land, and our masters make it almost impossible to do so.'

Friar Tuck jumped up, his round face solemn for once. 'Of course you must live on the land. Who does all the work, after all? You do. Who collars the result? These fat-bellied barons. They must go!'

Alan was on his feet now, his eyes shining in the

fire-light. 'That's right, my friends. They must go. Lock, stock and barrel. We mustn't rest while there's a master in England. All men equal from sea to sea!'

'Nonsense!' shouted a third speaker. 'What do you take us for? We're outlaws, aren't we? Our hands against every man? Isn't it hard enough to scrape a living for ourselves? Aren't there enough knocks without taking every serf's trouble on our own shoulders?'

There were murmurs of approval at this. The man looked round triumphantly.

'There'll always be masters – and good luck to 'em. Where'd we be, without rich men to pluck?'

He sat down amid applause. Robin stood up, a faint smile of contempt playing about his lips.

'We are not birds of prey, my friends – except by compulsion. I, for my part, would sooner eat honest food than live on carrion. Where shall we be when there are no rich men and no masters? Back at our work, my friends, whatever it is! Living in safety and comfort, not shivering and cowering here. Didn't we all come to Sherwood because we had to – like our friend here? Isn't his quarrel ours, and our fight his? If we all stand together we can beat D'Eyncourt. Some day we can clear England of masters from sea to sea.'

'Yes, we can – and will!' yelled Alan.

'We must work slowly, though. To begin with, we must teach the peasants to think as we do. And we can teach them by deeds better than words. We must help them against Sir Rolf in every possible way.'

And Robin, having won over the more doubtful outlaws to his plan, proceeded to describe the form it would take. It was put into practice the very next day, and before long Sir Rolf was wondering what devil of discord had been let loose within his domain.

A sudden change had overtaken his serfs. From being humble and timid, they had gained a new confidence, which at times bordered on defiance. He caught them grinning behind him as he rode through his fields. They had something up their sleeves....

One village had been behind-hand with its work. He determined to teach it a lesson, and the whipping-posts were set up on the green. Next day he would watch the culprits publicly beaten by his men-at-arms.

That night the posts were tarred and burnt. He found nothing but charred stumps when he arrived. Furiously, he demanded the doers of the deed, but no one knew anything about it. He picked on a man he suspected and sent him off under guard to the castle, to be hanged forthwith from the battlements. Then he rode on to watch the gathering of the harvest.

Somehow the man never arrived. The escort told a strange tale of unseen enemies who had showered arrows upon them from the forest. Their captive had vanished in a moment and a silver horn had been heard retreating.

Then there was that business of the lord's barn at Oxton. Master William, the bailiff, had been instructed to gather in every bushel of corn he could screw out of the people. If they went hungry during the winter, they could tighten their belts. Sir Rolf wanted the wheat!

On the very night that the barn was crammed to overflowing with the golden grain, a lurid glare crimsoned the summer sky. When Master William, cursing at being roused from bed, arrived with his guard, the villagers were working hard to extinguish the flames. No one could say they were not. They were rushing about and shouting, and tripping over each other, and spilling the precious water-buckets – but somehow the fire was gaining every minute. Master William took charge of operations, but it was too late to save the barn. Everyone went back to bed looking the picture of misery.

Next day, walking over the warm ruins, he wondered. There didn't seem much sign of all that wheat which had been burnt. The peasants seemed to be sharing some secret joke. Perhaps they were sharing something else? Perhaps they wouldn't be so hungry this winter, after all.

All through harvest time and afterwards it was the same. Things kept happening, and, for various reasons, it never seemed possible to bring the culprits to book. If a man was suspected, he either got mysterious warning and disappeared before he could

be arrested, or he escaped before he could be punished. Sir Rolf might set up gibbets and whipping-posts, but within twenty-four hours they would be burnt or sawn through. His men no longer dared to ride alone. They trusted neither the temper of the peasants nor the unseen bowmen in the woods.

Sir Rolf lived in a perpetual state of anger, as continual reports were brought to him of some new trick played on his men.

'Am I lord of my own lands or not?' he would thunder, banging his gauntleted fist on the hall-table. 'Parade thirty archers and thirty men-at-arms. I'll show them!'

He rode out at the head and they marched all round the villages. Men were flogged savagely at every halting-place; one or two were hanged without trial or preparation from the forest trees; fines and punishments were dealt out right and left.

'Kneel, curse you! Lower! Off with your cap!' With long, twirling whip he rode through the fields and lanes. At his passing, everyone had to kneel, the men baring their heads. Sir Rolf could not see their eyes, smouldering with anger and hate, bent on the earth which owned them, instead of their owning it....

'That's the way, William. The strong hand, the mailed fist. No nonsense –'

Thump!

A three-foot arrow struck him, piercing his silken surcoat, but rebounding from the armour beneath.

'Over there!' he bellowed. 'Search the undergrowth. Have him out – alive!'

His soldiers scattered and obeyed his orders.

They came back empty-handed. The unseen archer had left no trace. One of them picked up the fallen arrow.

'This is an outlaw's shaft, sir –'

'An outlaw's? Ah! I think I know who is at the bottom of this. I'll attend to him.'

His mind full of fresh plans, Sir Rolf rode grimly home. By the next day all Sherwood knew that the Lord of D'Eyncourt had been shot at on his own lands. Surely, some change was coming....

Chapter Eleven

Sir Rolf Goes Hunting

New things were stirring around Sherwood. Horsemen rode hither and thither at full gallop. D'Eyncourt Castle hummed like a hive. A thousand new arrows had been sent for and the armourers were busy repairing helmets and damaged links of mail. In every village and at every crossroad round Sherwood it was proclaimed that a bigger reward than ever was set on Robin Hood's head. Any outlaw who would betray him should have a free pardon.

No one came forward. At least, there was one man, an old soldier-of-fortune, not one of the band, but one of the solitary cut-throats who haunted the forest.... He was unwise enough to boast in an alehouse that he was on his way to the castle to claim the reward. An hour afterwards he was found dead in the ditch, his skull smashed by a peasant's spade. There were no more traitors after that.

News came every day to the outlaws' hiding-place. Robin sat in his cave, piecing together the bits of information as they arrived. Once, one of Sir Rolf's messengers was captured, but after that they rode always with a strong escort. The message that time was to a baron on the far side of the forest, asking him to guard all roads leading from Sherwood.

'They mean to hem us in on every side,' said

Robin quietly. 'Then they'll work through until they find us. The forest's not so large it can hide a hundred men – and there are the women and children to think of, too.'

'Let's get out while we can,' urged Little John. 'A quick dash, before the cordon's complete. We can be in High Peak in no time. If they chase us there, we can go to Barnsdale and the mountains. They'll never find us there. But Sherwood's too small.'

'You're right,' Robin agreed sadly. 'I hate leaving these folk, but there seems nothing for it, for the present. We'll hide all we can't carry with us, and move at sunset.'

There seemed no alternative. They were not strong enough to meet a determined assault from a force such as Sir Rolf could raise. With their retreat cut off, the band would be broken up and many lives would be lost.

No one was more sorry than Dickon as they packed up their few belongings and got ready for the night march. Though one of the newest recruits to the band, he had grown to love this spot. Besides, it was bad to be going away so far from his own village, and to be leaving Sir Rolf with a free hand to treat people as he liked. It was running away. Not like Robin.

He said as much to Martin. The ex-apprentice laughed bitterly. 'It's this or nothing. Do you want us to be caught like foxes, every earth stopped up? Do you want to dangle from the arm of an oak?'

It had been decided to break from cover on the west side of Sherwood. A short forced march would take them into the heather-clad hills and wooded dales of Derbyshire, where their enemies would have to begin the whole game of encircling them again.

'Ay, it'll be good to get in the heather again,' said Little John, homesick for his native moors. 'There's space to run in there, if you keep clear of Castleton.'

As soon as dusk began to fall, the long column formed up, women and children in the middle, and moved off along the secret forest trails. Scouts were spread out in front, making sure that the roads were clear. Dickon went ahead with Alan and a half-dozen others.

He had never been on this side of Sherwood before. It was hillier, a foretaste of the region where – if they were lucky – they would sleep tomorrow night. But first there was a strip of cultivated country to traverse, a tract of fields and dwellings where danger might lurk.

The forest thinned. 'About time too,' muttered Alan, 'if we're all to be out by dawn. The main body must be a good hour behind us. We come to a ford soon. Robin wants us to cross and hold it.'

'Surely we can beat off anyone who attacks us?' said Dickon. 'There won't be a whole army awake at this time of night.'

'We can't stand against horsemen in the open. And there are the women.'

In silence they continued on their way. Soon they gained the bank of the river, and found where the sandy track disappeared into it.

'Brrh! It's cold.'

'Shut up!' hissed Alan, splashing ahead.

When they were nearly waist-deep there was a sound from the undergrowth of the opposite bank.

The man next to Dickon gasped and fell backwards. Thinking he had slipped on the stony bottom, the boy put out an arm to help.

Plop! Plop!

Several crossbow bolts splashed in the water.

'Back!' yelled Alan, and the outlaws turned. Some slipped forward and swam, both for speed and to present a smaller target. Dickon followed Alan's example of wading as fast as he could, holding his bow up to keep it dry.

They regained the forest minus two of their number. From behind trees they peered back at the innocent-looking ford. At no point was there a hint of the concealed crossbowmen. They were being paid in their own coin with a vengeance.

'Run back to Robin, Hal,' ordered Alan. 'Tell him the ford's held. If there's another way over, tell him we'll distract attention here while he gets through with the main body. Then we'll join him in Derbyshire – when we can.'

The remaining outlaws strung their bows and waited patiently. After a time there was a stir among the bushes opposite. Three arrows sped and the sound of a fall rewarded them.

There was a suspicion of daylight over the forest behind when Robin arrived, panting, with a party of the fleetest men. 'There's no other way,' he gasped. 'Sheepford's guarded and the bridge is within sight of the castle. We must force a crossing here if we can.'

Half the outlaws stood ready to shoot at the first movement of the enemy. The rest drew their swords and, at a signal, dashed into the water. Dickon was among the first.

Thud! Thud! Plop! Plop! Thud!

A hail of bolts met them as they reached the middle of the stream. Over their heads the shafts streaked in counter-attack. Man after man slipped, groaning under the surface, and was carried away, bobbing and sinking in the grey water.

Dickon reached the shallows, Alan at his side, Little John rushing in front with a huge two-handed sword. With a cheer they ran up the bank.

A group of men jumped to meet them. Spears lunged at them, swords wheeled brightly above their heads. Cut and thrust and parry! The outlaws fought like demons, not only for their own lives, but for those of the whole party behind them. They must carve a way through.

Their comrades, no longer able to shoot safely, had plunged into the river and were crossing to their aid. In another minute the ford would be won! Alan was singing exultantly as he fought.

Then came a distant rumble, the drum-drum of hoofs. A strident horn rang out, and again nearer.

Foaming horses in the dawn light! Tossing manes and pennons, gleam of mail, rolling eyeballs –

The horsemen of D'Avaly!

Little John standing like an oak against a whirlwind.... Outlaws scurrying back like autumn leaves on the forest floor.... Robin's silver horn recalling them, the forlornest music that ever ear heard....

Dickon saved his skin with the rest, swimming downstream a hundred yards, with the icy water stinging a bleeding shoulder, while the horsemen rode into the shallows and cut down the hindmost. Surely Little John was down? But no, the Derbyshire giant was stalking back at his own pace, his great sword cutting an arc of death which warned his enemies to keep back.

Luckily, they were not strong enough to follow the outlaws into the forest. They settled down to guard the ford and sent patrols up and down the bank in both directions. Robin led his diminished party back to join the main body, and there, as the sun rose, they held a dejected council of war.

They were trapped. Already they had lost fifteen men, and this was only an indication of how they would fare at any point on the fringe of the forest. The whole countryside was roused. Every baron had agreed to guard that part of the forest boundary adjoining his own lands. Escape to the wider spaces of the Pennines was impossible.

Meanwhile, a swift rider was taking the news to Sir Rolf. Over his breakfast in the hall of D'Eyncourt, he heard how the outlaws had fared in their attempt. He laughed and called to his squire.

'Today we go hunting. Oliver, There will be good sport, I promise you.'

From the roof of the keep the rallying trumpet rang out over the castle. Archers and spearmen ran to arms. Horses were saddled. When Sir Rolf rode out over the drawbridge, two hundred and fifty men tramped after him.

The hunt was up! And a long-legged shepherd boy was racing to Robin with the news.

Chapter Twelve

Death Shadows

Sherwood Forest ran twenty-five miles from north to south. At its widest, it extended for about ten. This area was cut up into sections by the several roads which crossed it in various directions. There were hamlets, like Edwinstowe, right in the heart of the forest, and here whole acres of land had been cleared.

Sir Rolf's plan was simple. He would take each section of the woodland separately. His horsemen would patrol the roads all round it, while his footmen acted as beaters. When that section was searched, they would move on to another, and so, covering every inch of the ground, they would at last run the outlaws to earth.

If Robin attempted to slip back into a part which had been already 'beaten', the horsemen watching the roads could not fail to see him crossing, and warning would be given by trumpet-call and messenger. It seemed that now, after defying capture for a lifetime, the famous outlaw was doomed.

Meanwhile, the comrades were taking counsel what to do. Back at their old headquarters, they had rekindled the fires for breakfast, and were discussing whether to make a last stand together against three times their numbers.

'We've armour stowed away,' said Little John. 'We can fell some trees for a barricade –'

'That's it. Die fighting!' said another. 'We've got to die some day, and we couldn't die better.'

'Half a minute,' interrupted Robin with a smile. 'Why all this hurry to be dying? It's much more important to keep alive, not only for our own sakes, but for the people who look to us for help.'

'What else can we do?'

'Put our faith in Lincoln green and long-bows once again, not bother about armour and barricades! What do men call us? "Sherwood shadows!" We'll be shadows today – shadows of death.'

Quickly, for there was not a moment to lose, he unfolded his plan, which was quickly agreed to. The women and children hid themselves in the farthest recesses of the caves, where it would be unlikely that anyone would penetrate. Ten archers hid in the trees nearby, with orders to decoy the searchers away as soon as they came in sight.

Sixty or seventy men remained. They were split into parties of half a dozen or ten, each under an experienced forest fighter. Dickon and Martin attached themselves as usual to Alan's contingent. In five minutes the whole band had melted into the greenwood, and not a twig snapped as the parties trotted to their stations.

Sir Rolf, in the meantime, had ridden through his village of Oxton, and was preparing to draw the first covert. Chatting gaily, like sportsmen before a hunt, the mounted gentlemen scattered in groups along the road. From the other side of the wood, a mile or so away, the foot soldiers moved slowly forward in a fan-shaped open formation, weapons at the ready.

Half an hour elapsed. It was slow going through

the tall bracken and the dense holly-thickets. Men behind kept shouting to their fellows not to go so fast. They had to turn aside and plunge their spears into the thickest clumps, lest a man might hide there. At last they emerged on the high road, where the knights and squires were shifting impatiently in their saddles, their fingers itching on their sword-hilts.

'No one there, sir,' reported the captain of the men-at-arms. He turned to reform his company. After a minute or two he looked round with a puzzled expression. 'Four men missing, sir!'

Sir Rolf raised his shaggy eyebrows. 'Missing? How's that? Every man was to keep his neighbours in sight.'

'Yes, sir. We kept a ten-pace interval. But it's very hard to see all the time, even at that.'

'Oh, well, they'll turn up. I'll send them after you. Now we'll do this wood. Tell the men to keep each other in sight all the time. Let them talk. Then they'll notice if anyone drops out.'

The long line of soldiers moved across the road and was swallowed up amid the trees. The horsemen galloped round till the whole wood was completely encircled.

After a long interval the crackling of brushwood was heard, and shouts, both frightened and angry. 'I think they're coming,' nodded Sir Rolf. 'Draw swords. Ready –'

But the men who burst from the woods at that moment were clad in D'Eyncourt livery, and their faces were yellow-pale as their tunics. Two of them were carrying a body which they laid in front of Sir

Rolf. It was the captain of the guard. An arrow was buried between his shoulder-blades.

'Shot through the back, my lord,' faltered one of the men. 'We had cleared every inch of the ground behind us – yet shot through the back.'

'Anyone else missing?' barked their master. He rode up to the straggling line of sullen, fearful-looking men who were clustered along the fringe of the wood. Voice after voice shouted the bad news. Eight other men had failed to come through the wood alive. Yet no one had seen them die. With an oath, Sir Rolf bade them search the place again. There were some he had to drive back into that sinister patch of forest with the lash. Shot through the back. Already there were murmurs of treachery....

So the strange hunt continued, nor did the mounted hunters entirely escape. There was one impatient young knight who shouted that he had seen someone flitting through the trees, and urged his horse forward in pursuit. Only for a moment did his companions on the roadside lose sight of him, yet when he galloped back it was as a corpse, swaying in the saddle with a gash across his throat. They rode to the spot, saw the hoof-marks in the loose sand, but no trace of a human footprint.... Were they fighting against devils or men?

Dickon heard the hunt slowly approaching. He was glad. It was cramping work, lying along the stout arm of an oak, thirty feet from the ground, hardly daring to shift an inch. His bow was ready strung and he held an arrow between his teeth. Robin had said one shot each would be plenty, so long as it found its mark.

Voices were growing louder, he could hear the crackle of brushwood as heavy boots trod it down. The men were talking and shouting to keep up their courage.

'Fair gives you the creeps!' grumbled an unseen spearman almost below him. Dickon peered down and caught the gleam of helmet through the thick screen of leaves.

'No,' answered an archer close at hand. 'You never know who's going next, do you?'

'Poor old Ralph. He was near to me as you are, yet when I looked round he'd gone! Just like that. And when I went to look for him, there he was in the bracken, dead as mutton.'

'It just shows –' began the archer mournfully, but his sentence remained unfinished.

'Help!' said the spearman.

Dickon could see neither of them now, but he guessed what had happened. He drew his arrow back to his ear.

The spearman came into view, glimpsed through a gap in the foliage. 'Here, Hal, Giles, come here! They've got him! They've got old –'

High in the oak-tree something rustled, scarcely louder than a falling leaf. The soldier reeled, clutching his neck, then toppled over like a chessman and lay still. Dickon drew another arrow from his quiver, in case of need....

Three or four men came rushing in answer to the shouts. He saw them bend over the dead spearman, heard their exclamations as they noticed the body of the archer as well. He could easily have accounted for another of these silly gaping soldiers, who stared in every direction but the right one, but Robin had told them not to kill for the sake of killing. All that was needed was to work on the nerves of the soldiers, until at last they would refuse to enter the thickets, and the search would come to a standstill.

That time was drawing near, as he could tell from the muttered conversation of the men below. Thirty or forty of their comrades had perished in the dark corners of the forest and no one had so much as caught a glimpse of the enemy. It must be the work of evil spirits, not of outlaws. Only the arrows had to be explained somehow....

Suddenly, Dickon, intent on hearing every word, lost his balance. His bow went hurtling earthwards, and he himself, still clinging to the slippery bough, slid round until he hung face upwards. There he stayed, unable to regain his former position, and hanging on for dear life.

'What was that?'

The men were staring up at him. At any moment he expected to feel a crossbow bolt in his back. He clung to the bough desperately with closed eyes.

'Only some bird, Hal,' said another of the men. 'You've got the jumps. There's nothing there.' And they moved on out of sight and hearing, to catch up with the rest.

Dickon scrambled back and lay gasping along the arm of the tree. Luckily, his bow had caught in the lower branches and been hidden from view. If it had reached the ground, it would have betrayed the whole plan to the enemy.

The hunt moved away northwards. He heard occasional bugle-calls, then silence. Stiffly, he slid down the trunk and joined the others. Their work was over.

All day Sir Rolf searched the forest, but sunset found him with half his task untouched, fifty of his men gone, and the rest mutinous. In a black temper, he ordered his trumpeter to sound the recall.

Far away, silvery and mocking in the dusk, Robin's horn rallied the outlaws.

Sir Rolf heard, and cursed bitterly, as he rode home along the darkening roads.

Chapter Thirteen

A Dream for England

Dinner at D'Eyncourt was a mournful enough function that night, for Sir Rolf's mood was not improved by having his meal six hours after the usual time. But rejoicing and merriment were plentiful elsewhere.

Numbers of people, serfs and travellers, had seen the expedition trailing home with its tail between its legs. The news had spread. Over a hundred cottage fires the peasants were chuckling over their lord's discomfiture, and those who had a gift for song were already weaving fresh ballads of how Robin Hood had outwitted his enemies.

Even Nottingham had heard the news, brought by a passing horseman before night fell. There was laughter and jollity in Master Pole's house and in many more that stood round Weekday Cross.

Sherwood itself rang with the sounds of feasting. Once more the great central fire blazed in the heart of the forest and freshly-killed venison turned on the spits. The outlaws had dug up their hidden stores of ale and mead, and everyone was in the best possible humour.

'Eat, drink and be merry!' cried Dickon, his eyes dancing in the firelight.

'For tomorrow we die,' added Martin.

'Don't be so cheerful, Ginger,' retorted Dickon, pulling his hair.

'Well, it's true, isn't it? We go on like this, year after year, until sooner or later we get in the way of an arrow or a lance-point, and then – poof! Every outlaw ends like that, sooner or later.'

Dickon said nothing. He was sobered for the moment, thinking of those comrades who had died at the ford earlier in the day. What Martin said was true enough....

It was quite good fun to be an outlaw for a time, but how would he like it, year after year, winter as well as summer, never knowing any safety or any comfort? It wouldn't be so fine when he was Robin's age, or when he got rheumatics, as Friar Tuck did in the winter damps....

Hang it all, that would be years yet! Let's have another horn of ale, and show them all what a man he was.

Alan was playing his harp, as only Alan could. His fingers, twitching the strings, touched the hearts of his listeners too. You felt a queer lump in your throat at his music. Sometimes it made you want to get up and march and fight against all the barons in the world, and other times –

Robin stood up. The harp quivered into golden silence.

A hush fell on the ring of red, healthy faces.

'Friends –'

How they rose to him, and to the word! And he was their friend, not chief, like the leaders of most outlaw gangs.

'Once more we have beaten off the attacks of our enemies –'

'Ay, that we have!' There was tumult for a minute

before he could continue. 'Some of you are asking: how much longer are we to skulk in the forest, robbed of half the things that make life worth living? When are we going to strike back? My friends, the time draws near.'

Dickon was hanging on every word. He strained forward, cheeks ruddy with ale and excitement. What new plan had Robin up his sleeve?

'We have won the goodwill of the peasants and of the town workers. We have proved to both that we are not common cut-throats, but their fellow strugglers against the power of barons and kings. The time is nearly come for them to join the struggle openly – and it is our privilege to lead them.'

He paused and looked round. Every face, old and young, was as intent as Dickon's. There was no doubt of their faith and enthusiasm.

'All men are equal in the forest,' went on the outlaw. 'They should be equal in the whole world. They should work for themselves and for each other – not for some master set over them. Let the ploughmen plough for all and the weaver for all – but let no lord step in to steal the harvest and no merchant prince to take the cloth. Then the common people will have twice as much as they have now, and there will be no more hunger or poverty in the land.'

No more hunger, no more poverty! Dickon's heart sang. It was all so clear. Of course it could be so, once they got rid of lords and abbots and their bailiffs. Why hadn't anyone seen it before?

'There must be an end of serfdom!' Robin's voice rang clear above the crackling fire. 'An end of tolls and tithes, and dues and forced services! The land for the peasants and the town for the workmen! No more castles, no more hired cut-throats in livery, no more war service, no barons, no king!'

'No baron! No king!'

The very forest seemed to echo and re-echo the cry. Dickon and Martin shouted as loudly as any.

Robin flung back his head and laughed, his pointed beard lifted to the stars. Every outlaw in the band was behind him, he knew. He had made them see the dream which had been his for years. He lifted his hand and they were quiet again.

'It won't be easy, my friends – if it was, we'd have done it long ago. It takes years to persuade men, to show them the one truth – that there are only two classes, masters and men, haves and have-nots. Everything else – Normans and Saxons, Christian and Saracen, peasant and craftsman – is a means of keeping us apart, of keeping masters on top.

'Well, people hereabouts are beginning to see. For years we've befriended the villages. We've brought them to understand. And some of the Nottingham folk too. When the hour strikes, they will all rise together – and the power of D'Eyncourt, ay, the power of the King himself, will crumble before them.'

'How?' shouted someone eagerly.

'Because without the peasants, the barons cannot live. They would starve. And if the peasants turn and fight, no army can stand against them. Why, half the soldiers are born peasants themselves. They will join their own flesh and blood to overthrow the tyrants.'

Robin paused, his eyes reflecting his triumph.

'Can we do it, d'you think?' whispered Martin doubtfully.

'Of course!' hissed Dickon. 'We can do anything.'

'The people must stand together, that's all,' said Robin.

'The barons may be too stupid to stand together on their side, but in case they do, we shall plan the revolt for winter.'

The boys wondered why. The outlaw went on to explain.

'The roads are at their worst then and the fords impassable. It's the hardest time of the year for the barons to move their armies about. If half the shire rises, we can settle our own masters before their friends in Yorkshire and the other parts can send help. By the time they get on the move, they'll have enough to do with their own estates.'

Once more his laugh rang out exultantly.

'We'll light the flame in the Midlands, my friends!' he cried. 'But it'll spread, north and south, east and west, till all England's ablaze. The people will rise in a great host, and no strong place will hold out against them. And when the last castle has hauled down its flag, we shall build the new England, the England of equality and freedom – Merrie England at last!'

Chapter Fourteen

An Abbot Ambushed

They must have money. And that autumn saw the band gathering money as greedily as any miser.

They must have money. If the revolt was to succeed, it would mean leading armies of peasants and workmen away from their homes for weeks, perhaps months. They would have to be fed during that time, or they would grow discontented and sheer starvation would break up their numbers. And there must be no desertion, no drift back home, until the fight was won.

Rich merchants began more than ever to avoid passing through Sherwood. With uncanny knowledge, the outlaws always managed to be there in time to rob them, however secret they had kept their journey. And all their gold and silver went into the growing hoard in Robin's cave.

Small game, this, and not enough to satisfy the needs of future armies. So Robin departed on a mysterious mission to Nottingham; Little John went off to Hathersage, to prepare the men of Derbyshire for what was coming; other outlaws vanished on various business, until less than twenty were left in Alan-a-Dale's command at headquarters.

'Just our luck!' grumbled the friar at breakfast one morning. 'Here's a fellow brings word that the Abbot of Rufford is going off to Lincoln tomorrow with hundreds of pounds – and we're too few to do anything about it. We'll have to let all this good money go by.'

'I'm wondering,' mused Alan.

'You can go on wondering,' broke in Will Scarlett. 'How do you think twenty of us can rob the abbot on the main road, with folk passing all the time? He travels with a dozen armed guards when he's got treasure.'

'If only we could get him off the main road....'

'If!' jeered Will. 'Go up to him and ask him to come into the forest for a moment, eh? "Won't you walk into my parlour, said the spider to the fly?" Where's your brain, Alan?'

'Its usual place. Tuck, you old humbug, you know something about the Abbot. What would tempt him?'

'The Abbot of Rufford,' said the friar solemnly, 'cares for two things above all else in the world – and we have neither to offer him.'

'Cleanliness and godliness – I don't think!' interjected Will.

'No,' retorted Tuck. 'Money and pretty girls!'

There was a roar of laughter. 'That's stumped you, Alan,' cried someone. The harper rubbed his chin thoughtfully.

'I don't know. Dickon here would make a very good girl, if we dressed him in some of those fine clothes we took from the merchants' bundles last week.... We've everything else we need, now – some horses, saddles, armour, livery –'

'Whatever for?' they shouted together.

'You'll see. Leave it to Uncle Alan!'

So it was that the Abbot, riding along next day with his escort and treasure-train, was respectfully accosted by a squire, behind whom a little group of riders was halted, bearing arms and colours he could not remember having seen before. To increase the Abbot's interest, one of the riders was a slim girl, modestly veiled.

'Pardon me, my lord,' began the squire humbly, 'but my master is dying close by. He wants a priest so that he can confess his sins –'

'Is that it?' snapped the Abbot ill-temperedly. 'I am in a great hurry, sir. Can't you find a parish priest? He doesn't need an Abbot, does he? My time's very valuable.'

'I am sorry, my Lord Abbot, but my master is in great trouble. He has, during his life, collected great wealth and wide lands – not always by honest means. His conscience is pricking him. He would like to leave half his possessions to some religious house, some abbey –'

'Ah!' said the Abbot genially. 'That's different.'

'He thought perhaps one of the abbeys in this shire where he is dying. Newstead, possibly, or –'

'Rufford? What's wrong with Rufford?'

'I think your lordship's advice would quickly persuade him.'

'So do I,' answered the Abbot dryly. 'Who gets the other half?'

'His daughter here. She would be the ward of the said abbot until she married, and the abbot would... look after... her inheritance for her.'

'He would.' The Abbot's tone was enthusiastic now. 'Where is your master?'

'About a mile – down that by-road –'

'I don't like by-roads. Still, with your men and mine – yes, it should be safe enough. Lead on, sir. I will ride with the young lady and – er, comfort her.'

It was lucky that Dickon's knobbly brown hands were hidden by gloves, for the Abbot spent a good deal of his time patting them as they rode along, and might otherwise have noticed something strange.

'You must be very beautiful, young lady,' he murmured. 'Such graceful fingers can only go with a lovely face.'

'Do you think so?' simpered his veiled companion. 'Perhaps, when you see my face, my lord, you may not be so pleased with it.'

'Nonsense!' cried the Abbot gallantly. 'I can tell that you are as beautiful as you are ... er, good.'

'That's about right,' mumbled Dickon under his breath.

'What's that? I didn't quite catch that.'

'I am sorry, my lord. I was only praying for my poor father. Oh, oh, oh!' He bowed his head and sobbed realistically.

'There, there, little girl,' protested the Abbot comfortingly.

'I – I'm not – a – a – little girl, at all.'

'Of course not. You're quite a grown-up young lady. Don't cry. I'll look after you.' His fat face became almost roguish and his small eyes twinkled with mirth. 'I expect you and I will get on very well together, my dear.'

Occupied as he was with this pleasant conversation and his own even pleasanter thoughts, the Abbot did not notice how far they were going down the lonely by-road. At last he glanced round him, however, and called to the squire who rode in front: 'How much farther, my friend?'

'Just round the corner, my lord.'

'All right. I'm quite happy.'

Dickon caught the signal in Alan's look. 'Forgive me, my lord,' he murmured, 'I must hurry to my father.' He spurred forward and vanished round the bend. Hampered as he was by his clinging dress, it would never do to be caught in the midst of the Abbot's men at the critical moment.

Now the little cavalcade rode into view, Alan and his six men in front, the Abbot, his chaplain, his twelve retainers, and the pack-horses behind.

'What's this?' exclaimed the Abbot. 'I see no one. You said –'

He stopped, ashen pale to the lips. The seven disguised outlaws had wheeled across the road, their lancepoints twinkling wickedly in a row.

'What's this?' cried the Abbot again. 'Draw your swords, men. There is something –'

'Stop!' interrupted Alan. 'The first man who moves will get an arrow.'

Half a dozen more outlaws, in the familiar Lincoln green, slipped from behind trees and covered the escort.

'It's a trap, my lord!' burst out the chaplain in agitation. 'Turn your horse, and make a dash –'

'Look behind you,' cried Alan. They turned their heads. Across the road stretched another line of bowmen, their shafts ready on the string.

'Horsemen,' ordered the outlaw. 'Draw your swords – no, one at a time – and throw them in a heap. You first, then you, and you, and you.... Right. Now come forward, dismount, and wait. Anyone who moves –'

There was no need for him to finish. Their faces, as they eyed the archers, showed that they understood perfectly. The Abbot alone remained on his horse, his eyes rolling this way and that in fear.

Tuck and two other outlaws came forward and led the pack-horses into the forest. No one else moved, until the last sound of hoofs and crackling brushwood had ceased. Sherwood had swallowed the treasure and the Abbot knew better than to hope he would see it again.

A long whistle, as from a sentinel, broke the stillness. 'Someone coming,' said Alan pleasantly, 'it's time we were leaving you, my lord.'

'Just a moment, Alan!'

Dickon rode forward and lifted his veil enticingly. 'Won't you kiss me goodbye, my Lord Abbot?'

Everyone roared with laughter, even the Abbot's men, and his own chaplain could not repress a snigger. The fat face purpled with anger.

'I'd like to –' he spat venomously.

'Come, darling,' laughed Alan, seizing Dickon's hand. The archers backed slowly into cover, and within a minute not an outlaw remained in sight.

Secret Service

'You seem pretty good at disguise,' said Robin with a smile. 'First, the weaver's apprentice then the knight's daughter.... Yes, I think you've got a better chance of pulling this off than anyone else in the band.'

'I'll do my best,' muttered Dickon huskily.

'It'll be dangerous –'

'I don't mind. What am I this time? And where am I going?'

'A page. And you're going to – D'Eyncourt Castle!' Dickon's jaw dropped. 'But I'll be recognized at once –'

'No. For you're going on Christmas Day. The castle will be packed to overflowing. There'll be half a dozen barons there as guests, and no one will know whose page you are. And when Alan's finished with your face and hair, none of the D'Eyncourt people will know you from Adam.'

'What am I to do?'

'Mix with the crowd – and keep your eyes open. Note the fortifications, especially the alterations Sir Rolf has made since he came home. Fix it all in your head, so you can draw it for me with a stick in the sand. Look out for weak points. See how the entrance to the keep is defended –' Robin rattled off a whole number of things he was to look out for. At the end he said: 'A great deal depends on you,

Dickon. We are going to take D'Eyncourt Castle. The flames of its burning will be the signal for all England to rise.'

Take D'Eyncourt!

Dickon remembered the boast with dismay as he drew near those grim walls a fortnight later. How could the outlaws and peasants, without any of the engines of war, prevail against a fortress of such size and strength?

He passed, with a stream of other people, into the outer ward. It was Christmas morning. The outer ward was thronged with peasants gathered to stare at the gentry, with entertainers who had come to perform in the great hall, and with beggars, cut-purses, and anyone who saw a chance to profit in so large and varied an assembly.

No one took much notice of the smart page, who, with bleached hair curled and trimmed, and the smartest of doublets and hose, walked disdainfully through the crowd.... He must be in the train of some lord or other. Had been sent out on an errand, no doubt....

With a beating heart, Dickon stepped on to the drawbridge.

Even the outer ward, intended for the safe keeping of cattle, was strongly defended by a ditch; and would offer considerable resistance to an enemy. But the castle proper began only with the drawbridge, and the twin-towered gatehouse which Sir Rolf had rebuilt in the latest fashion of fortification, How could Robin and his comrades ever batter it down?

A deep moat, covered with ice, lay beneath the beams of the bridge. He measured it with his eye.

Twenty feet across, at least. Then the bank rising steeply, and a high stone wall on top of that. It must be sixty feet to the battlements, if it was an inch.

Now he was passing through the gate, into the long, narrow passage under the gatehouse. A portcullis hung at both ends, each a heavy spiked grille, designed to strengthen the iron-studded gates. A casual glance upwards showed him the 'murder-holes', through which any invader trapped in that narrow corridor could be speared or shot from above.

It was a relief to reach the open air of the inner ward, where the old oblong keep carried Sir Rolf's

banner sixty feet above the grass and flagstones of the courtyard.

At this moment, the guests were streaming out of the chapel, a lower building close to the north wall, where they had been attending Mass.

'Eh, lad, you'll cop it, won't you?' said a burly Yorkshire man-at-arms at Dickon's side. 'Missing chapel, eh? What'll your master say? Who is he?'

'I was on an errand for him, fellow,' replied the boy with great dignity, moving away before any more awkward questions could be put.

Sir Rolf was leading the way up the covered staircase into the keep. Behind him came a procession of lords and ladies in their festal finery, with a sprinkling of priests. The lesser folk, such as squires and pages, servants and musicians, brought up the rear. Dickon mixed with these, his mind and tongue alert for any answer that might be needed if he was spoken to. Meanwhile, his eyes searched the staircase. He must remember everything....

A gate at the bottom, with a portcullis. Twelve low steps. A landing, but, before you got to that, another gate. Twelve more steps, and a third gate, before you came into the keep itself. A good place for a last stand!

Robin had told him to look out for weak points. There weren't any! D'Eyncourt could defy an army.

Racking his brains for a plan, he moved on into the banqueting hall. Sir Rolf and his guests were already seated on the platform at the far end. Men were carrying in the boar's head, geese, capons, and other delicacies.

Dickon thought of his own family, shivering in

their hut, but thinking it wonderful to have a little extra today. Yet these men and women at the high table were guzzling as though their lives depended upon it, and throwing meat to their hounds which would have fed dozens of hungry humans.

He sat down amid a group of chattering pages, and began to eat. He might as well enjoy his Christmas, anyhow, even if his life was in danger every minute. Nothing like this in Sherwood today – just the same old venison, with a stolen chicken or goose thrown in. He had never seen such a spread as this in his life.

'Have some wine,' said his neighbour affably. A goblet was thrust into Dickon's hand, and he took a deep gulp. Then he spluttered and they all laughed. He was not used to this hot, highly-spiced liquor. He must be careful. It would go to his head.

'Drink up, man!' cried the other page impatiently. Dickon drained the cup, and it was refilled.

'Haven't seen you before,' went on his new friend. 'Who are you with?'

Dickon paused. To gain time he buried his nose in the goblet and took a long drink. Pages took a pride in knowing all the different families, their titles and coats-of-arms. If he lied, he might get himself into a mess. . . .

'I say, who are you with?' repeated the page.

Dickon eyed him stupidly. The only thing to do was to pretend drunkenness. 'Why, I'm wi' you, of course. Who d'you think I'm with?'

The other pages roared with laughter at his clumsy humour. But it did not amuse the youth at whom it was aimed. He flushed angrily.

'Don't get cheeky with me, my lad. Don't you know I'm the senior page here? I shall be a squire next summer.'

'Thash nothing,' retorted Dickon thickly. 'I may be – only a page now – but I'll be a whole book someday.'

'You'll be a corpse more likely.'

'Oh, leave him alone, Etienne,' interrupted another lad. 'Can't you see he's drunk? Fancy getting drunk on two cups!'

This time the laugh was against Dickon, and Etienne joined in. Suddenly he leant forward and muttered to the other page:

'All the same, there's something queer about him. Two cups of wine don't make your hair change colour.'

'What do you mean?'

'Look behind his ear. There's a curl of black hair. The rest's light gold.'

'Perhaps he wants to be in fashion,' said the other lazily. 'Ladies like blond boys now.'

'I'm going to tell Sir Denis.' Etienne slipped from his seat and strode towards the high table.

Dickon thought quickly. He must get out of the hall. If he was haled up to the high table, Sir Rolf would pierce his disguise at once. He rose, overturning his stool.

'Here, just a moment!' said the other page, his tone more serious now. Fortunately the table was between them.

'I – I think I'm going to be sick,' mumbled Dickon. There was another roar of laughter as he fled, stumbling over dogs and elbowing the servants by the door.

As he gained the head of the staircase, he heard Sir Rolf's bellow from the far end of the hall. It was neck or nothing now. He fairly flew down the broad flight of steps.

There were plenty of people in the courtyard. He mingled quickly with the stream. In another moment he would be over the drawbridge....

'Close the gates!' The order rang out from somewhere behind him. To his horror he saw the gates swing into position, and the sentries stand to arms. He was trapped.

Where could he hide? He looked this way and that. Everyone was staring round, asking what was the matter. He had just a moment before the search began.

The chapel! That was the one place sure to be empty. He slipped round one of the wooden sheds which served as soldiers' quarters, and ran for the arched doorway. Behind him a confused hubbub arose as the men-at-arms began to push through the crowd, asking questions and peering into faces.

In the chapel it was quiet and very dim. It was also very bare. Where could he hide if they came to search? He peered round anxiously.

There was no safety between the round pillars – a torch would pierce that shadow in an instant. There was no hiding-place anywhere. And he could hear the rumble of voices, distant, but coming gradually nearer.

Ah, there was a hiding-place! High in the air, just under the roof itself, great beams of Sherwood oak stretched from wall to wall. And here was a winding staircase leading to the bells. Perhaps he could manage somehow to scramble on to one of those beams.

It was a perilous business. At one moment he thought he could never make it. He was spreadeagled between a ledge and the beam, unable to go forward or back. Far below, the hard stone flags waited for him to crash to his death.... A supreme effort carried him to the beam, and he fell flat along it, choking with dust and cobwebs, just as the chapel-door was opened and a crowd of men poured in.

'He must be in here, then!'

The hushed voices floated up eerily to the listening boy.

'Unless he got out before the gates were shut.'

'Well, if he didn't, he won't now. If he's anywhere in the castle, he'll be caught sooner or later. Everyone is being examined before they're let out. He won't get through.'

'All the same, we'll have a look around.'

Judging by the time taken, Dickon thought the 'look round' a very careful search. He heard the men come up the belfry stairs, felt them in the darkness close at hand, peering along the criss-cross rows of beams, and scarcely dared to draw breath. At last their footsteps retreated, the door closed, and for the moment he was safe. But how on earth was he going to leave the castle?

If everyone was to be examined, asked their name and business, he would never get past that gate-house. His hair alone would give him away. Curse that unruly black curl, which Alan must somehow have missed!

The gate was no good, then. What about the

walls? A forty-foot drop, then the steep bank and the moat.... If he could get a rope, perhaps under cover of darkness he might do it.

But again how? If he began searching the sheds for a forty-foot rope, he would be almost certain to be seen. He had no idea where one might be stored. Likely as not, he would walk into the soldiers' quarters by mistake.

Fool, why hadn't he thought of it before? The bells, of course!

He rose carefully on the beam and, heart in mouth, regained the ledge. There he sat, watching the thin streaks of white light made by the windows, until they slowly changed first to grey, then to utter darkness, and he knew that the short December day was over.

This would be as good a time as any. The soldiers would have had their dinner by now, and everybody would be stupid and sleepy with over-eating and drinking. Most of them would have crammed into the hall to hear the musicians and see the acrobats.

He drew his dagger and began to saw through one of the thick bell-ropes. He judged it would be long enough. If not, he must drop the rest of the distance.

The last strand parted. The rope hissed down through the darkness and curled itself like a snake upon the flags. He groped down the stairs, straightened the coils, and slipped it over his shoulder.

One moment! He must not let Sir Rolf know that a spy had been in D'Eyncourt. He must do something to throw them off the scent. Let them think it had been a thief.... He ran to the altar, picked up two of the gold candlesticks, and thrust them under his doublet. Then cautiously, inch by inch, he opened the door.

Snow was falling – that would help. Lights gleamed from the slit-windows of the keep. The inner ward was empty. Keeping in the shadow, he made for the battlements.

Luckily, the outer ward lay on only one side, not all round. A single wall and the moat barred his escape at this point. With trembling fingers he knotted the rope round a projection, and again it hissed down through the air.

Footsteps! A rough: 'Who's there?' Someone running, and a gleam of armour in the starlight.

Dickon swung himself over and slid.

The end of the rope rushed through his bleeding fingers. He dropped like a stone. How much farther – five feet or fifty?

He hit the bank and rolled over. The back of his head struck the ice of the moat. Dizzy and shaken, he sprang to his feet.

A crossbow bolt thudded against his shoulder, and the whole arm went numb with pain. He set his teeth and scrambled up the bank on the other side.

Several men were shooting from the battlements. He saw their heads, black against the sky.

'A merry Christmas!' he yelled back scornfully, and bolted for the safety of Sherwood.

Chapter Sixteen

When Sherwood Rose

'We can never take a keep like that,' said Robin decidedly. 'Unless we can think of a trick....'

There was silence for a few minutes while everyone thought furiously. 'I know,' cried Alan. 'We've been planning all wrong – thinking of the keep as the last place we have got to capture. It's got to be the first.'

'But how can we get at it?'

'Dickon got into the castle and hid, didn't he? Why shouldn't others? During the day, when people are going in and out freely, half a dozen of us can enter as pilgrims or something. They can hide in the chapel – along the beams.'

'Go on,' urged Robin. 'This sounds all right.'

'Then, in the night, you start your assault from outside. We can safely reckon that Sir Rolf will put every man on the outer battlements. There'll be no one in the keep because no one will be needed there. That's our chance – those of us inside – to nip into the keep and lower the portcullis of the staircase. Then they can shoot at the defenders from behind.'

'It's chancy,' said Little John slowly. 'If there are any men left in the keep....'

'We'll deal with them.'

Dickon begged hard to be one of the party. As he knew the lie of the land, they reluctantly consented. Otherwise, they felt that he had done his share, and that another attempt to enter D'Eyncourt might be very dangerous for him. Dickon pointed out, however, that the only people likely to recognize him from his latest escapade would be the two pages, who would have left by the time of the revolt.

Meanwhile, there was much to be done. Mysterious messages were passing through the countryside, whispered from serf to serf. Everything had to be ready for the rising which should end the power of the masters for ever.

The twelve days of Christmas feasting ended. The barons rode away with their own retainers through the January drizzle. A red-dipped arrow passed secretly from hand to hand.

A party of story-tellers and singers came to the castle. Eager for anything to break the winter monotony, the household and garrison crowded into the hall to hear them. One by one, ten figures slipped stealthily into the chapel. One was a peasant who had brought in eggs; another was a strolling friar; others had come in with the troupe of players. All had mail shirts and swords under their clothes, and one humpbacked boy, who had staggered in under a great load of firewood, carried long-bows and arrows concealed within the bundle. Only two outlaws had failed to reach the chapel. They had been disguised as beggars, and the sentries had kept them out.

All through the day they sat or stretched themselves along the high beams. The castle chaplain pattered the evening services down below, unconscious of the waiting men above. Curfew was tolled, nearly deafening them. Night settled on the castle.

They came down, stripped off their robes and

rags, and groped for their bows. Dickon slipped off his 'hump' with a sigh of relief and swung his quiver on his back instead.

'When we go,' whispered Alan, 'Ulric and Gurth had better stay here. Sir Rolf may try to make a stand in the chapel, if he can't get into the keep. So bar the door after us. You can shoot from the top windows, and, if they do get in, you can hide on the beams again.'

No more words were spoken. They waited breathless in the dark.

Ha-haa!

Robin's silver horn, very faint in the distance. A shout from a sentry, a bugle-call from the gatehouse –

'Someone coming!' hissed Alan. 'Stand still in the shadows.'

The door opened, a man showed for a moment against the lesser darkness outside. They heard him grasp the bell-rope and tug.

Clang! Clang! Clang!

The harsh alarm-bell awoke all the echoes. Suddenly its measured ring stopped, dying away in a succession of lesser beats. The ringer slid to the floor with a knife-thrust in his heart.

'Follow me,' said Alan.

Soldiers were pouring across the courtyard. Torches danced and flared. Arrows seemed to be falling from the sky, and every now and again a man cried out, or slumped to the ground in a writhing heap.

'Every man to the ramparts!' came Sir Rolf's bellow. He had armed himself in a couple of minutes, and now came striding across with his huge two-handed sword over his shoulder.

Someone passed, shrieking: 'The outer ward's gone! It's the serfs! Thousands of them –' Sir Rolf swore, and began to run towards the gatehouse, as fast as his heavy mail would let him.

In the confusion, the outlaws themselves, mailed and steel-capped, passed without any recognition. As they neared the entrance to the keep, the last of its defenders streamed down the steps to take their places on the outer wall.

'Now!' cried Dickon exultantly.

They shut the bottom gate and lowered the portcullis. Both the other gates they locked and barred behind them as they climbed the stairs. Except for the women and the chaplain, they had the keep to themselves.

'Two stay and guard the door,' said Alan. 'One of the women might try to open it. The rest of you, follow me to the roof.'

Snatching a torch from its socket, he led the way, sword in hand. There seemed no end to the winding steps. They passed the hall, the hall gallery, and the dormitories, catching a glimpse of women who screamed and fled at their approach. At last they came out on the battlements under the open sky.

From the outer ward rose a fierce red glow as the barns and stables went up in flames. The gatehouse towers stood out clear and black against it, and they could see the backs of the defenders as plain as day. They were pouring a hail of arrows, bolts and stones upon the unseen attackers, but it was evident that they were suffering themselves.

Taken by surprise, they had not time to fix the wooden boardings which usually added to the protection of the battlements, and the keen shooting of Robin's men found many a mark.

'All the same,' said Alan. 'They'll never capture the gatehouse like that. Robin said he'd have ladders ready on the north side. That's where we can help.'

For the present they held their fire. It was not long before a rush of defenders to one point on the north wall showed that an escalade was to be attempted. Normally, this was one of the hardest ways of attacking a fortress, and Robin would never have attempted it but for his allies within.

Great cauldrons of boiling oil and water were sizzling on the ramparts. Huge stones were being dragged along and balanced on the embrasures, ready to be cast down on the heads of the attackers. Crossbow-men were shooting as fast as they could wind their weapons, but, luckily, this was much more slowly than a long-bow could be bent. Soon, a louder roar than ever from the attackers, answered by the jeers of the defenders, showed that the moat had been filled and the first ladders were now going up.

'Pick your men, and shoot,' said Alan briefly.

Six shafts whizzed from the roof of the keep. Several of the defenders crumpled up.

'Fast as you like!'

The outlaws stood grimly along the wall, shooting as rapidly as they could draw back their strings. Every man who lifted a ladle of oil or put his hand out to push one of the stones over dropped, as though by magic, where he stood. There was a whole heap of dead before the survivors realized the new quarter from which they were assailed.

'Treachery!'

The cry ran and swelled into a roar. White faces, distorted with rage and fear, turned upwards to the keep. A shower of bolts rattled on the battlements, and one of the outlaws jumped back with a gasp of pain. A band of men at an order from Sir Rolf, ran across the yard and began to batter at the bottom gate of the staircase.

Meanwhile ladders had been planted at two points. Hindered as they were by the volley from the rear, the defenders were unable to dislodge them. Men began to swarm up and, for the first time, Dickon saw the attackers.

Serfs they might be, but tonight had transformed them into heroes. They surged over the wall, their red faces set under the steel caps Robin had given them. The first few were as well armed as their enemies. After that came the men with scythes and pitchforks, hammers and staves, and wooden boards for shields.

Terrible carnage was wrought on that slippery ledge. Man after man fell, grappling with his adversary, and rolled to the grass of the courtyard below. The outlaws on the keep could no longer shoot into the mass, so they turned to pick off the reinforcements who ran to the spot.

Below them, a loud crash signalled the forcing of the lowest gate. Would the others hold long enough? If Sir Rolf regained the keep before Robin entered the castle, the lives of the six outlaws would not be worth a farthing. Meanwhile, a cloud of missiles swept the roof, and for whole minutes they could not show their heads to shoot.

Fifty of the besiegers had gained a footing on the outer wall. Forming into a compact body, they began to move round towards the gatehouse. The defenders assailed them savagely behind and in front, and archers poured their bolts into them from the courtyard below. Their ladders had been thrown down, no reinforcements could come from outside, and they were cut off.

It was touch and go.

Ulric and Gurth appeared suddenly on the roof of the chapel, and caused a diversion by shooting down from a fresh angle. But they were only two....

'No more arrows,' snarled Alan. 'That settles it. Out we go!'

Feeling that they were going to almost certain death, the little party quitted the roof and ran down the winding stairs. 'Open the door,' said Alan to their two comrades at the bottom. 'Bolt it behind us. Keep them out as long as you can.'

With drawn swords, they went down to the second gate, which was quivering under the impact of a ram. 'Now!' whispered Alan.

The door swung back suddenly. The attackers sprawled inwards on the top of the beam they carried. Before they could recover, the outlaws were on them, hacking and stabbing....

'Now for the gatehouse!'

With dripping blades they issued into the courtyard. 'Sherwood!' they yelled, defying the cries of 'D'Eyncourt!' and raced across the yard.

An archer, dagger in hand, spun on his heel to meet Dickon who struck blindly and ran on. There was a mist of battle-madness before his eyes, and he could see nothing but the dim towers of the gatehouse looming in front.

Surprised by this new attack, the defenders did not realize how small the party was. Men ran hither and thither in panic, not knowing where to turn. The keep, the chapel, the north wall – everywhere the rebels were in possession! And now they had reached the gatehouse... the inner portcullis was slowly rising!

Above the din of battle they heard a song. The men who had sung so often as they toiled at their work for Sir Rolf were singing as they turned the winches in his gatehouse. And now the gates stood open, the drawbridge was down, the main body of the besiegers was pouring into the inner ward!

Dickon found himself glaring into the eyes of Master William. For the first time in his life he was able to meet that gaze, and to know it was the man, not himself, who was afraid. Their swords crossed, the bailiff rushed on, trying to overbear the youth by superior weight.... He took Dickon's sword full in the face, cried out horribly, and crashed to the ground.

An hour later the flames of D'Eyncourt were added to the glow of the sunrise. Sir Rolf never saw them. He lay, weighed down by his armour, at the bottom of the moat, where Little John, with an immense back-handed blow, had sent him from the battlements.

But all Sherwood saw that second sunrise, made by the burning of their tyrant's stronghold. They took it as a sign of the new dawn. Through every hamlet ran the word:

'Sherwood, arise! The time has come!'

Chapter Seventeen

Gathering Clouds

'You realize what this means, Your Grace?'

Earl and Archbishop faced each other in the narrow room. The priest made no answer. His fat white fingers drummed nervously on the table.

'It means,' went on the Earl, 'the end of you and me. If this kind of thing goes on, my castle will go the same way as D'Eyncourt. And you, Your Grace, will dangle from the gateway of your fine palace at York.'

'It can't go on,' muttered the old man, his face the colour of dirty parchment. 'God won't allow it –'

'God didn't save D'Eyncourt,' laughed the Earl sardonically. 'It's not angels we want, but archers.'

He paced the room in silence, his brow black with anger. The Archbishop turned in his chair. 'What's the news this morning?' he quavered.

'That serfs from all over the shire are flocking to his standard. He has an army of five thousand men – some say ten thousand. And he intends to march on Nottingham.'

'This is very dreadful, very dreadful indeed.'

'Say something new, for heaven's sake! You make me sick. We must do something.'

'Put the town in a state of siege?' suggested the priest timidly. 'Surely that rabble – you don't think they could get at us in the castle, do you?'

'State of siege!' jeered the Earl. 'And let the whole country rise from Kent to Cumberland – while we're bottled up in here?' He banged the table with a heavy fist. 'See here. This revolt has got to be crushed – instantly. Wiped out even from the memory of men. Otherwise, we can never sleep safe in our castles again.'

'Yes, I – I see that. But what can we do?'

His companion took a deep breath, as if striving to be patient with a child. 'It's lucky I was here,' he said. 'No one else seems to have an idea how to manage things.'

He walked to the window and peered through the slit at the town below. The market-place was full of people. Talking about the revolt, no doubt. Sedition. He shouted for a guard. 'Tell the captain on duty to clear the market-place with horsemen. Arrest any-one who talks about Robin Hood. Or knock them on the head. That's simpler.'

He turned back and faced the Archbishop. 'I've sent out messengers,' he said softly. 'Troops are coming from all over the midlands. In three days I shall have six thousand men in Nottingham. By that time there will be another army of five thousand at Newark. We shall advance from opposite directions and catch this rabble in the jaws of the pincers.'

'A splendid plan! You are a great general, Wessex.'

'I have some sense,' said the Earl sourly. 'I know that this thing has got to be nipped in the bud, or it is goodbye to all our power. How would you like to work for your living, Your Grace?'

'Er – is there anything I can do?' said the old man, changing the subject quickly.

'Yes. Issue a proclamation through every priest and bishop in your province. Say that God ordained that men should work for their masters, and anyone who says differently will go straight to Hell. These ignorant ploughboys will believe you. They'd believe anything, if an Archbishop told them. That should make a lot of them desert and stop a lot more from joining the revolt.'

'I'll do that, then.'

'And drop a hint to every monastery that we don't want anything about this put in the records. I'm going to stamp it out – utterly. Then our sons and our sons' sons won't have the same thing again.'

'Can you – utterly?'

'I think so.' The Earl smiled to himself. 'I have sent word in every direction. The roads are closed. No one can carry the news south or north. The rest of England knows nothing.'

'It will get through all the same.'

'Of course! A whisper or two, a rumour. But by that time it will be all over. Dead men tell no tales. And the people of the north and south will never know it really happened. Leave it to me.'

There was a rap on the door. A messenger saluted. 'The manor houses of Grenfleld and Outshaw are taken by the peasants, my lord.'

The Earl whistled. 'You see, Your Grace?'

'Dreadful, dreadful,' wailed the old man. 'Have these men no gratitude to their masters?'

'They are not men. They are vermin. They must be treated as such. Any more news, my man?'

'There are rumours from Derbyshire, my lord. They say that the manor of Hathersage has been taken by serfs.'

'And what of the rebel army?'

'Nearly a thousand peasants marched in yesterday from the neighbouring estates. He has fully seven thousand now, and five hundred are mounted. Many are well armed. Apart from the arms they have captured, they must have had many hidden beforehand.'

'They must! It's unbelievable. They've mail, they've lances – they've money. There's a brain behind them.'

'The outlaw,' put in the Archbishop.

'I expect so. Ah well, we'll deal with him. I'll spill those brains myself with my battle-axe.'

The Earl went back to the window and looked out. What he saw made him chuckle with satisfaction.

The townsmen were falling back before his riders. This time they had no Sherwood archers to help them. The square was dotted with dead and dying, among whom even women could be seen. The horsemen rode backwards and forwards, cutting down everyone in their path.

'That's the way,' he murmured approvingly. 'After all, they're freemen. It's not as though they were serfs and belonged to any of us. Ride them down!'

'What is it?' said the Archbishop suddenly. 'What is it that makes these men fight back when they haven't a hope of victory? They die like flies on your swords, yet they seem to die gladly.'

'Perhaps –' The Earl hesitated. 'Perhaps it is because some day they know they will win. But not in my time,' he added quickly.

'That would be very dreadful,' agreed the Archbishop softly. He folded his chubby hands on his stomach and thought of dinner-time.

In the market-square below they were dragging away the dead.

Storm Breaks

'They've swallowed the bait,' said Robin triumphantly. 'There they go. The road is clear to Nottingham!'

They were standing, Robin and John, Alan, Dickon, and one or two others, on a wooded hill three or four miles north of the town. Below them, screened from distant view by the trees, the peasants' army stood halted in its ranks.

Robin flung out his arm and pointed. A long column of men, their helmets and spear-points glinting in the winter morning sun, was winding across the fields and into the forest. Already its vanguard was lost behind the bare trunks of Sherwood, and as they watched, it slowly disappeared, coil by coil like a steel snake, along the northward road.

With a laugh Robin turned and ran lightly, despite his years and his unaccustomed armour, down the hillside to the dell in which the serfs were gathered. He jumped on a tree-stump, and everyone fell silent.

'My friends –'

A husky murmur of agreement ran through the ranks. 'The Earl of Wessex has marched past us. The town lies for us to take. There is only a small garrison there, and our comrades inside, the people of Nottingham, will open their gates to us. Within an hour we shall hold the town. By tonight perhaps –

who knows? – the strongest castle in middle England will be ours!'

There was a roar of approval, cries of 'Lead on!'

'Well, friends, who follows me to Nottingham?'

This time the answer was deafening. Swords, lances, axes, waved like a forest of saplings. Shields flashed like mirrors in the sunshine. Robin swung himself into the saddle and they marched after him like a trampling herd.

Yet there was discipline in this strange army that the genius of an outlaw had forged. Every man knew his duty and his place. Shadow-like as ever, the Sherwood men glided in front and on the flanks, spying out the land and watchful for an ambush. Alan and three hundred horsemen rode ahead to make sure of the town gate. Little John and the other mounted men brought up the rear. Dickon rode at the giant's side, still marvelling that they had ever found armour and a horse to match such a man.

'Isn't it splendid?' he cried impulsively.

'We're not out of the wood yet,' answered John dourly. 'It's all too easy to be true.'

'Croaker!' laughed the boy. 'I say, fancy me on a horse and in this armour!'

He bent forward and patted the dappled neck of his beautiful grey. It was hot and stuffy in this mail, and the helmet was heavy. Besides, the piece down the front to cover his nose made him go cross-eyed till he got used to it. Still it all made him feel bigger somehow, and stronger. He was glad he was used to horses, and had been made one of the cavalry –

'Now what's up?' boomed Little John. The

column in front had jerked suddenly into a quicker pace, which was almost a run.

'I say, look up there!'cried Dickon.

Slowly defiling over a ridge to their left was a strong party of horsemen.

'They must be some of the enemy from Newark,' said John. 'Hope there aren't many of them. Robin's trying to slip by. It's very dangerous.'

'They're getting ready to charge!'

'By thunder, they'll cut our column to ribbons if they do.' He turned in his seat. 'Ready, lads!' he roared to the men behind.

A rumble from above, as though the hillside were about to crash down on them. Then a living mass of men, horses, and steel, cascaded down like a mountain torrent.

'Charge!' countered John in a stentorian voice.

Unleashed by the word, the rearguard swept slantwise across the hillside. They struck the attackers in the flank, and on both sides the impact was terrific. Beasts and men tumbled and rolled over. Shields and lances shivered on one another. Added to the unholy confusion were the arrows poured into the thick of the fray.

Dickon found he had ridden through without a blow. He wheeled, with the idea of returning, and saw to his joy that the enemy were streaming back to the skyline, where they halted and reformed, remaining like a row of black statues brooding over the scene. His first cavalry skirmish was over.

Orders came back from Robin. They could not go forward with such a force on the flank. It must be dealt with first, before the advance on the town continued. The rebels accordingly fell back on a line of rising ground facing the ridge on which the enemy lay.

It was no cheering sight that they now saw. The force from Newark was still pouring over the horizon, and it numbered at least five thousand men, many of them mounted and all well armed. It would be a near thing....

'Stand fast, friends!' Robin encouraged his followers. 'Let them tire their horses first. Longbows can keep off horses, I'm sure. Then our turn will come.'

He placed his own two small mounted parties on the wings. For the rest, the spearmen locked their shields in a solid row, and the archers stood behind to shoot over their heads.

The assault came quickly. The barons and knights, eager to teach this rabble of ploughboys a lesson, thundered down their own hill and up the other side.

The shield-line never wavered. Few of the horsemen ever reached it. The arrows struck them like a blast of sleet. They bowed their heads to the feathered storm, tried to ride forward, died in heaps, were forced to wheel.... From Robin's horn came the two notes which John and Alan knew.

Once more the rebel riders poured forward like unleashed hounds. They curved across the slope like swallows, joined in the middle, and tumbled the retreating enemy down the hill. Then, in good order, they withdrew to the flanks again.

'That's taught them something,' murmured Dickon with the satisfaction of one who has just knocked a high-born youth over the tail of his charger.

'M'm,' said Little John. 'I think we can stave them off. But –' He stopped suddenly, staring northwards. 'Look there – it's Wessex coming back. Ride and tell Robin. Or we're done for!'

Dickon took one look at the approaching troops. There was no doubt. Somehow, word had reached Wessex. He had turned and was leading his six thousand men back on their tracks, to take the rebels in the rear. Every second, the jaws of the pincers were closing in....

He found Robin in the centre of the line. The outlaw's face was pale and set. 'That's not the worst news, Dickon boy. Tell John – no one else, mind – that we must stay here and fight it out, Wessex or no Wessex. Word has come from Nottingham. The plot has been discovered and the people taken by surprise. Their leaders are dead, hanged this morning. The town gates are closed against us.'

'Then – then –?' stuttered the boy.

Robin nodded. 'Short of a miracle, we are as good as dead men, all of us.'

'I can't believe it. Our cause is right. It must win.'

'Of course it must. But maybe not today. Maybe when we're all dead and forgotten, and Robin Hood is only a name in songs and stories. Go back and tell John. I – I'll try to see you both again.'

Dickon rode away, blinking back hot tears.

Robin came out in front of the little army.

'Listen! We are going to clear the hills opposite. Walk slowly and keep your ranks. Today will be the first great victory of the people. Nothing can stop us. Forward then! Down with the barons!'

Their voices were like the sea. And like the sea

they surged slowly forward, a rippling tide of steel.... Down one hill and up the other they marched, shoulder to shoulder, grim gaze fixed on that waiting line against the sky.

Twice the knights hurled themselves against that relentless flood. Once they broke the shield-wall. But every man who passed through was dragged from his horse and killed. The hillside was flowered with proud surcoats as well as common jerkins. Remorselessly, the tide lapped up the hill, ebbed and flowed forward again.

Surely it was the miracle of which Robin had spoken?

The peasants, with only the gallows before them, fought like furies. They flung the startled knights aside and came to the men-at-arms. The two masses grappled in a death struggle. Superior numbers told. The masters' mercenaries gave ground. It was not rout, but it was retreat.

Then, from a quarter of a mile away, the trumpets of the Earl of Wessex gave tongue. Their brazen sound rolled up the hill. The peasants, warmed with victory, felt suddenly cold. They all knew now that they were trapped.

Dickon had faced death often in the past few months. He was not afraid now. But if only he could have died in victory, instead of defeat! Had it all come to nothing after all? Would the masters go on being masters forever?

Robin spurred towards them. He smiled at Little John. 'Thought I'd like to be with friends,' he said. 'It's just a fight to the finish now. There aren't any orders to give.'

'Let's cut our way out,' urged John. 'There are other parts of England. We can start again.'

'They're coming,' interrupted Robin.

Once more the waves of horsemen broke on the solid ranks of the peasants. Once more the longbow tumbled baron and knight on the earth. But it could not go on. There was a gap. The tossing plumes were through.

'Sherwood to the rescue!' roared John. Waving his battle-axe, he swept into the thick of the fight, levelling every one who stood in his way. Dickon followed, hacking and slashing, wondering when his own death-blow would come.

The peasants were split into little groups now. It was happening as it had happened at Hastings. It would soon be little more than a massacre. The sunset itself was not so red as the hillside.

Tuck, Will Scarlet, a dozen old comrades he had seen go down. The worst shock was when Alan – Alan of the merry heart and happy music – grinned up at him from under his horse's feet... the grin of a dead man who would laugh no more.

A couple of foes made for him, one on either side. His arms were almost too tired to lift his sword. So this was the end! He felt one terrific blow across his head, and it was all over. He knew no more. Another body fell to be trampled with the rest.

North

Over his head the silver branches of Sherwood made a lace-like pattern against the pale blue of the February sky. Somewhere, birds were singing, just as they used to do before – before –. He rubbed his aching head weakly, trying to remember. Was he dead? Was this Heaven after all?

'You'll soon feel better,' said Little John, and his great cheerful face came into view, bending down from the sky to smile at the boy.

Dickon sat up. 'What happened? Where are we?'

'Back in Sherwood – for the moment. A few of us cut our way out at the last moment.' John's smile faded at the memory of that terrible scene, when the masters had taken full vengeance for D'Eyncourt. 'The darkness saved us. Many of us got away like that.'

'You saved me?'

'I could see you were only stunned. And you were no more than a featherweight on my horse. It was nothing.'

'Thank you,' said Dickon softly. 'What happened to Robin? Was – was – he –'

'No. Only wounded. He's over there. Gurth is binding his arm for him.'

Dickon looked around. There were nearly a dozen old friends, some attending to each other's wounds, others busied around a fire, from which a savoury smell of dinner issued. They were still wearing their mail and their steel caps, all hacked and dented and stained with brown which was not rust. They grinned back at him.

Back in Sherwood! It seemed too good to be true. Then he remembered Alan's face and the others', dead behind them on the battlefield. Nothing could be the same again.

'Well, lads, it's north now – fast as we can.'

Robin spoke, between bites of hot venison from a steaming bone he held in his fingers. They gathered round, listening eagerly.

'We'd be safe in Sherwood, of course. If we wanted to go back to the old game. But I've had enough of skulking in the woods. We're not beaten yet.'

'No!' chorused the outlaws.

'Yorkshire will rise to a man. They only want a lead. We were unlucky this last time. If the Earl hadn't been there, there'd have been a different tale. And Yorkshire will be another matter.'

'There's plenty of masterless men in Barnsdale Forest,' put in Gurth. 'As soon as they hear Robin Hood has come north, they'll come flocking in. We'll have another band, and within a year we'll be marching south again with a conquering army.'

Robin staggered to his feet. His face was drawn with the pain of his wound, but the old spirit shone from his eyes. 'We've no time to waste, then. North it is!'

They stripped off their armour and left it. The horses were turned loose, being useless in the country through which they must travel. For the last time, the men in Lincoln green went flitting like shadows through the glades.

Men were seeking them everywhere. The forest roads hummed with horsemen like bees in summer. And the wayside gallows were heavy as apple-trees in autumn, as dozens of serfs and outlaws were rounded up.

But Robin and his party escaped. They struck northwest, crossed the fields under cover of night, and reached the heather moors where Little John was born.

It was lucky the weather was mild, and there was a hint of spring already in the air, for otherwise Robin might have died in those bleak hills, where the Christmas snow still lay thick in the hollows.

How different it was from kindly Sherwood, this forest of the High Peak! All the trees were in the dales. On the starved uplands, where the outlaws spent most of their time, there seemed not a scrap of cover from the wind, and they could get no fuel for their fires.

They came down to Hathersage, a straggling mountain village with a church high on the hill above. 'That's where I was born,' said John fondly. 'And when I die, I reckon I'd like to be buried in that little graveyard.'

They dared not enter the village, but John and Gurth went down under cover of darkness and brought back such poor provisions as the inhabitants could spare – a scraggy chicken, some dried peas, and loaves of gritty black bread.

Next day they followed the River Derwent farther

and farther into the heart of the hills. The land grew bleaker and lonelier. Even in the dales, there were few trees. The river dwindled as they got near its source. The valley closed in on either side, until it was no more than a gorge. At last they struck off to the right, up a stony gully made by another stream, and mounted higher and higher towards the skyline.

'It's a great country,' murmured Little John. He strode in front with the long, tireless pace of the hill-man.

Dickon wished it were not so great. There seemed no end to it. Every crest they climbed showed them another and higher one ahead. On every hand the grey-green moor rolled away like a desert, broken only by strangely shaped crags and tors.

The trail disappeared. John, with all his moorcraft, had lost it. And now an element of horror was added to the journey.

Bog!

Suddenly John let out a yell of warning. His foot had gone right through the earth to the knee, and a pool of evil-looking liquid had bubbled up all round it. Dickon glanced instinctively at his own feet. They too were sinking. Water was creeping over his boot-tops.

With a cry of alarm, he jumped from the sucking moss to a spot of bright green turf near by. Too late he found that he had exchanged the frying-pan for the fire. The ground seemed to open beneath him. He was waist-deep in the chilly quaking bog.

He struggled, almost mad with terror, but his movements seemed to send him farther in. It was over his ribs, it was pulling him under. And the others were floundering about, fully occupied with saving themselves.

He tried to cry out again, but the sound was strangled in his throat. He was too paralyzed with fear to utter more than a husky gasp. He sank slowly, the slime sucking him down.

'Spread your arms out!'

It was Little John's voice, but how far away it seemed! Mechanically, Dickon obeyed. He put his arms out, and spread his palms downwards on the surface of the bog. It seemed to stop him sinking.

'Now catch hold!'

John's notched old quarterstaff was thrust into view. He clutched at it desperately.

'Hang on like grim death!'

There was no need for that advice. Shutting his eyes, Dickon fastened on that friendly pole like a leech. He was moving now. Slowly but surely, he was being drawn out of the mire. A few moments later, filthy and soaked from chest to toe, he stood on firm earth again. The bog gurgled as it subsided, like some foul monster disappointed of its prey.

At last they crossed that terrible range of hills, nearly dying of cold and hunger on the way. They came down into Yorkshire. Barnsdale was not far away.

Robin's wound was giving trouble. He would say nothing, but Little John knew it was not healing properly, and was causing him great pain. It needed proper treatment.

One day, when they were close to Huddersfield, the outlaw leader collapsed. They covered him with a blanket and took counsel together. It was clear that he was in a high fever.

'We must get him indoors,' said Little John decidedly. 'If he stays out here he'll be dead by tomorrow.'

'Where can we take him?'

'There's a convent at Kirklees, only a mile away. The nuns will take him in.'

'What about the price on his head – and ours?'

'We must chance that. The other way, he's sure to die, anyhow. And we can say he's a traveller, wounded by robbers. They won't know.'

An hour later the unconscious outlaw was carried through the convent gates, which he was destined never to leave alive.

Chapter Twenty

Into the Hills

Robin stirred on his bed in the guest-chamber of the nunnery. His fever had left him, but memories remained, like a nightmare, of what he had overheard as he tossed there in his struggle with death. They had thought him delirious – but he had understood enough.

'Yes, it must be Robin Hood.' (He seemed to hear the whispering voice now, to see the white, wild face of the Prioress bending over him in the candlelight.) 'He will live' (they had said) 'but we must keep him till they can send for him. A messenger has gone. Perhaps the Earl will give us the reward.'

Treachery! And in the very place where they talked most of goodness and truth! The sweat started on his brow. He was helpless in the hands of these women.

'Did you call?'

A nun came into the room and stood beside him.

'I want my friends, the men who brought me here.'

'That is impossible. No man is allowed within the convent. Had you not been dying, as we thought, we should not have taken you, even.'

'Then I'll go to them.' He strove to rise, but fell back panting. The fever had made him so feeble. 'I'll be better in a moment.'

'But you can't. The Prioress –'

'I will.' The woman flinched at the tone, still hard as steel, despite the speaker's frailty. 'Two of you can help me to the gates. Then my friends –'

'I must tell the Prioress,' she exclaimed in alarm, and rustled from the room. It was some time before she returned, followed by the Prioress herself.

'Of course you shall go,' said that lady soothingly. 'Just rest a few moments to get your strength, and then we will help you up. Look, I've brought you a drink of wine.'

He drained the cup in silence. New warmth flowed back into his veins. He felt better already. He closed his eyes for a moment. He must gather his energies together, and in a few minutes he would walk out of this place for ever.

The time passed. His eyes did not reopen. He was sound asleep. The Prioress smiled.

'Just the thing to do him good. But he must be bled again.'

'Madam!' The nun's voice was shocked and amazed. 'The fever has quite left him. Surely it is not right to bleed him now. It is most dangerous –'

'So you know better than I?' The Prioress's tone was icy. Her smile had changed to a mask of hate. 'I have nursed and doctored for thirty years. Of course, we all make mistakes. If I make a mistake this time... I shall be very sorry.'

Without another word, the nun brought the bowl and other necessaries. The Prioress rolled back her sleeves and set to work with the deftness of a surgeon.

'There now,' she said at length. 'I'll be back in a

moment to stop the bleeding. He'll be ever so much better when he wakes. When he wakes!'

She was gone. The nun sat watching. Robin slept on, while his life's blood drained away into the bowl....

It was time the Prioress was back. But there was no footfall in the passage. This man never should have been bled at all. If it went on for another minute, he would die from loss of blood.

Terrified, the nun realized what she had known all along, but had not dared to admit to herself. The Prioress was not coming back. Rather than let the reward slip through her fingers, she would – do – this.

Murder!

Her hands flew to her cheeks. Her eyes grew large with horror. No! No! Not even if he was an outlaw. She couldn't. Sooner would she defy the Prioress.

Hastily she bound up the wound and stopped the flow of blood. Robin gave a contented sigh. It was an hour before he opened his eyes. The Prioress was beside him, and the room was full of nuns.

'I'm dying?' he said calmly. She bowed her head. Tired as he was, his brain worked quickly. There was still a chance. He would never give up hope. If only he could get out of this den of women, into the forest, he would grow well again. He must play-act as he had never done before. He clasped his hands on the coverlet and pretended to pray. Then at last he said meekly:

'I should like to be buried near here.'

'That wish shall be respected,' answered the Prioress with a secret little smile at her own thoughts. She knew that Robin would never be buried. His head would be set on the gate of Nottingham, his body hacked in quarters –

'I should like to shoot once more. Where my shaft falls, there let my grave be.'

'There is no harm in humouring him,' muttered the woman. So they brought his bow and arrow, and raised him up so that he might aim through the narrow window. For the last time he bent his bow, but he had not strength to draw back the arrow right to his ear. 'Bad shooting,' he said wistfully, as it sped. 'However, it will serve.'

Little John, waiting in the bushes outside, saw that shaft, and ran to pick it up. There was no message tied to it as he had hoped, but it told him enough. He shouted to the others and they ran to the convent gate.

'Robin's in danger! We've got to get him out, if we smash the place down.'

Crash!

He hurled his immense weight against the doorway, but it did no more than quiver under the impact. A terrified woman peered through the grating and vanished.

'Fetch a log,' bawled the giant. He hammered on the gate like a madman. The sound echoed and re-echoed through the cloisters and corridors within.

'Here we are,' shouted Gurth. 'Swing it up, lads. All together!'

Bang! Bang! Crash!

The hinges gave. The stout door fell flat and they leapt over it, plucking their swords from their sheaths.

Ha-haa!

Was it imagination, or was that the feeblest of horn blasts from an upper room? It had just the silver note, but it was so soft and weak –

Little John mounted the steps four at a time. He burst into the room to find Robin alone. The nuns had fled into hiding when the door was broken down.

Dickon was close behind. He stopped in the doorway, uncertain, half-ashamed. Because Little John was crying like a child.

Dickon felt rather like that himself. His mouth opened and shut, but he couldn't speak.

It was Robin now who looked like a baby, because John had swung him up in his arms and was carrying him out and downstairs, as though he weighed no more than thistledown. Dickon sheathed his sword and followed, wondering what would be the end of it all.

They paused on the first hilltop and laid Robin down. He was dead. Gurth spat savagely. 'So they got him in the end. They always do. Well, we've paid them for it.' He glanced back at the Priory, from the roof of which smoke and flames were rising.

They buried him in a wood, cunningly, because his enemies would not let even his dead body alone if they find it. Then they stood up, dusted their hands, and looked at one another.

'This is where we part, I reckon,' said Gurth. 'I'm going south again.'

'I'm for Barnsdale as before,' said another.

'I'm sick of England. I'm going to try Ireland.'

Little John and Dickon found themselves alone. 'Looks as though we're the only ones left who care much about Robin's ideas,' said the boy wistfully.

'Yes. I reckon things will come about slower than we thought. Perhaps not in our time at all. But we'll do our best. Robin was right, dead right.'

'An England without masters,' murmured Dickon, looking towards the hidden grave. 'Sounds daft, doesn't it? But he was right. He dreamed, when the rest of us couldn't see further than our noses.'

Little John put a hand on his shoulder. 'Shall we go south together, Dickon boy? Back to the High Peak? I don't fancy Sherwood again now, somehow. What do you say?'

Dickon took the big hand and shook it. 'Right, John. And we'll go on working to make Robin's dream come true.'

Two figures slipped southwards, mere shadows in the wood, their faces set towards the Derbyshire hills.

Author's Note

This story was first written in 1934. As a boy in Nottingham, playing with bow and arrows in the park which is still called 'the Forest', I always thought of Robin Hood as my favourite hero. But growing up and learning more about life, I felt that some of the stories did not ring true. The 'jolly outlaws' could not have found things so jolly, really, and a man like Robin would not have been so ready to fall on his knee before the King. So I tried to create a new picture of Sherwood Forest which should be truer to life.

Not everyone liked my new picture. It is, of course, 'only a story'; but so are they all, for there are no certain facts about Robin in the history books. Yet there is nothing impossible about this tale, even the idea of Robin leading a great rebellion – such a thing actually happened in 1381. In fact, throughout English history many men thought of him as that kind of person. When Walter Raleigh was on trial in 1603, he cried out: 'For me, at this time, to make myself a Robin Hood, a Wat Tyler, a Kett, or a Jack Cade – I was not so mad!' All the other three men actually led great revolts in England, so Raleigh must have thought of Robin as a similar leader.

Luckily, there were many others who welcomed the book. Boys and girls wrote to me from all over the world. Some could not because they did not know a word of English – they were reading the story in their own languages in Italy and Poland and Brazil. It was even turned into Icelandic. A friend told me how, when fighting in the Spanish Civil War, he found a German translation of it in Barcelona which had been published in Russia.

This was my very first book. I have written nearly sixty since then. So when at last this story went out of print in English, after nearly thirty years, I hesitated before consenting to a new edition. It is a young man's book. If I were writing it now I would write it rather differently. I have learnt a lot (I hope) since those days, about historical details and many other things. But I also know that there are some things (like running upstairs) that a young man does better than an older one. People, in England as well as in far-off countries, seem to want the story, and a very discriminating critic, Margaret Meek, has said that as 'a clear yarn it has still much to offer', so here it is.

I was lucky in that Mr C. Walter Hodges, one of our outstanding modern illustrators, whose work I have always admired, agreed to do the pictures for this entirely fresh edition, and caught so sympathetically the atmosphere I had tried to create. Otherwise, I have taken the opportunity of changing a few words and phrases here and there, but, as I have just explained, it remains essentially the first book of a young man writing long ago, and I think it would be a mistake to make any wholesale revision.

G.T. 1966

YOUNG SPITFIRE'S

The White Camel by Eden Phillpotts

Set in the Arabian desert, this tale of physical and spiritual growth stirringly captures the adventures of Ali, a Bedouin chieftain's son.

from Joanne Harris's Introduction:
'I can't tell you how happy I am that this magical book is finally going to be made available once again... It is a wonderful book for adults and children alike, with a style which manages to be both intensely poetic and excitingly muscular at the same time. It is good to see a children's book written without a hint of condescension or any taint of political correctness. ...It is also a terrific adventure story in a kind of Arabian Nights tradition.'

ISBN 1 904027 25 3   192pp   Paperback   £9.99

The Viper of Milan by Marjorie Bowen

Set in fourteenth-century Italy, the story is about the enmity between two princes, Visconti, the evil Duke of Milan and Mastino della Scala, the dispossessed Duke of Verona. The hatred of these two men is the absorbing basis of the plot, but the vivid descriptions of Milan and the countryside, and the almost unbelievable cruelty and black-heartedness of the unscrupulous Visconti, help to make the impact of this story a really tremendous one.

ISBN 1 904027 24 5   274pp   Paperback   £9.99

John Diamond by Leon Garfield

Narrated with verve and pace by a master story-teller, John Diamond follows the quest of William Jones and his heart-stopping adventures through the streets of a richly-imagined eighteenth-century London. With a cast of characters worthy of Charles Dickens, 'John Diamond' was the winner of the Whitbread Award and the Boston Globe–Horn Book Award.

ISBN 1 904027 32 6   208pp   Paperback   £7.99

A selection from Leon Garfield's

JOHN DIAMOND

My father made his fortune in London. He'd been in coffee – not like a spoon, but in the way of buying and selling it, in barrels and sacks. He never talked about his years in trade, which consequently gave them an air of mystery and romance, with a strong sensation of ships.

He never really talked much at all; or at least, not to me, except to remark on my dirty fingernails and to ask me if I intended to grow up to be a sorrow to my mother and a disgrace to my sisters, who always nodded as if they fully expected that to be the case.

Yet, like everybody else, I couldn't help liking and admiring him, and would have done anything to earn his praise. I would lie awake at nights, dreaming of distinguishing myself in every possible way – except, of course, the one that would have pleased him most, which was to be clean, neat and studious, to follow in his footsteps and be a pillar of the community.

His footsteps! Now I've come to them. I hated and dreaded them. Every night I heard them, back and forth, back and forth across his room, which was directly under mine.

They started when the house was quiet, at about midnight, and went on and on until I fell asleep. Sometimes I tried to count them, like sheep, and then to work out how far they would have reached if they'd been laid end to end. I think it was to Edinburgh; but later I discovered that his journey was a good deal longer.

At first I thought he might have had the toothache; but, as his face was never swollen, and he had no trouble with eating, it was plain that the reason lay deeper than that.

I knew he was unwell. Dr Fisher from Hertford had called to see him several times, and had gone away looking glum; so it occurred to me that, just as some people have the sleeping sickness, some the falling sickness, my father had the walking sickness, and that was the cause of it.

If so, it was a very strange malady, for it only attacked him by night and drove him from his bed, to walk and walk, as if he would wear out a grave in the floorboards with his feet.

That he was as ill as that – to bring graves to mind, I mean – I first learned from Mrs Alice one Saturday afternoon in September, when the rain had kept me in.

Mrs Alice was our cook and housekeeper rolled tightly into one, and secured by an enormous white apron and a crusty white cap, so that she looked like a wrinkled old baby who had been left waiting at the font.

I was in the scullery, helping myself to raisin wine, which was kept in a stone jug covered with a bit of beaded muslin to prevent the flies.

She came in so suddenly that I had no chance to escape and could only stand, with the jug up to my face and the muslin veil on my head, waiting for her to shout loud enough for my father to hear.

Instead, she gazed at me mournfully and said it was high time I stopped thinking only about myself and began to think of being a support to my mother and sisters as my father could not live for ever.

A selection from Eden Phillpotts'

THE WHITE CAMEL

Sheikh Abbas was a mighty man of valour who lived in Arabia and reigned over a clan of the Bedouin Arabs, leading them from place to place with their herds and flocks. His people feared him, but they always obeyed him because he was not a person you could say 'No' to very easily.

Now, when I speak of Arabia and tell you that the White Camel lived all his wonderful life there, you will say, 'Which Arabia?' Because there are three. Arabia the Stony is a land of mountains and fierce wadis, or river-valleys, where the great streams roar down in the rainy seasons and dry up again when the sun comes out to roast the world; Arabia the Blessed is the land of cities and farms and fruit and oil and honey and corn and sweet scents that make the air delicious to breathe; and Arabia the Sandy is a vast and burning desert, where strange things happen and strange folk dwell. Mountains thrust up out of the great ocean of sand, and scattered upon it sparingly are oases and wadis, where the precious water rises from far below and gives the trees and shrubs and grass a chance to live and prosper in the midst of that thirsty world.

Now Sheikh Abbas dwelt upon Arabia the Sandy; but he had a beautiful oasis of his very own in the midst of it. When he and his people were tired of wandering upon the great Red Desert of Dahna – to find the browse that their sheep and camels needed – he would break up his camp and take everybody back to his oasis, that the men and women and children and flocks might see the green of living things again, and drink sweet water from the wells, and eat fresh fruits and enjoy themselves, before they set out once more upon their restless wanderings. For the roaming Bedouins cannot stop in one place very long: they must be on the move and they would hate to be like the townsfolk and settle down in one house for evermore. They better love to dwell under their tents and wander amid the adventures and dangers of the eternal sand.

And now you meet the little clan of Sheikh Abbas, encamped two days' march from the oasis, under a low ridge of hills that ran between them and the eastern sky. It is the middle of the night, and the moon shines above the desert and makes the sandy wilderness all grey. Far out in the desert hyenas are laughing together and making a faint but horrid noise. What they are laughing about nobody can tell you, but they are rude fellows, with rather nasty manners, and I don't suppose their jokes would amuse us very much. The desert jackals are also breaking the great silence. They howl in rather a mournful fashion and don't sound as if they had much to laugh about; but they annoy the dogs of the camp, and the dogs bark back at them and tell them to shut up and run away.

Where is the camp itself? But for an accident you would hardly see it, for it is crouching under the low, dark hills, and there beneath their little tents, woven of goats' hair all dyed pitch black, dwell a large company of men and women; while round about the horses, camels and sheep are herded. At this time, in the dead of night...

This edition published in
Great Britain in 2004 by

Elliott & Thompson Ltd
27 John Street
London WC1N 2BX

First published in 1934, revised 1966

ISBN 1 904027 26 1

First edition

Book design by Brad Thompson
Printed and bound in Malta by Interprint